The LEARNING RELATIONSHIP WORKBOOK

APPLYING BUSINESS PRINCIPLES TO STRENGTHEN RELATIONSHIPS

PRINCE-JAMES SMITH, PHD

THE LEARNING RELATIONSHIP WORKBOOK

This workbook is educational and reflective. It is not a substitute for therapy, medical care, legal guidance, crisis intervention, or other professional services. Readers experiencing relationship abuse, coercion, threats, violence, severe emotional distress, self-harm thoughts, or safety concerns should seek immediate support from qualified professionals, emergency services, or appropriate crisis resources.

Quantity sales and special discounts are available on quantity purchases by corporations, associations, and others. For details, contact the publisher at the address above.

Orders by U.S. trade bookstores and wholesalers. Email Michael@BeyondPublishing.net

The Beyond Publishing Speakers Bureau can bring authors to your live event. For more information or to book an event contact the Beyond Publishing Speakers Bureau speak@BeyondPublishing.net

The Author can be reached directly at BeyondPublishing.net

Manufactured and printed in the United States of America distributed globally by BeyondPublishing.net

BEYOND
PUBLISHING

New York / Los Angeles / London / Sydney / Bangkok

ISBN: 979-8-9962262-3-8

DEDICATION

For the dreamers at heart who are determined to be successful at love.

This workbook is dedicated to those who still believe that love can be strengthened, repaired, studied, practiced, and renewed. It is for the individuals who refuse to treat relationships as accidents of emotion alone and who are willing to do the deeper work of becoming more intentional, more aware, and more resilient in connection.

This is for the people who understand that lasting love does not survive by hope alone. It survives through presence, humility, responsibility, repair, and the repeated choice to show up. It survives through small actions in the present moment that move the relationship one step closer to trust, clarity, and shared strength.

Jonalyn, Isaiah, Kaleb, Dane, Addison, Ray, Jersey, Luke, Eliza, Hayden, Crystal, James, Brandon, the kids of the future. Go forth love with a skillful purpose.

This is for you.

ACKNOWLEDGMENTS

The work of building a relationship is never entirely individual. Love is shaped by the people who teach us, challenge us, support us, disappoint us, forgive us, and call us into deeper versions of ourselves. This workbook was created from that understanding. It reflects years of study, professional experience, personal reflection, business development, behavioral science, cognitive psychology, and the lived recognition that human connection is one of the most complex systems we are ever asked to navigate.

I acknowledge the scholars, clinicians, theorists, researchers, and practitioners whose work has helped shape the language of this workbook. The ideas of systems thinking, organizational learning, attachment, cognitive interpretation, behavioral change, dyadic coping, emotional regulation, and resilience have each contributed to the framework presented here. This workbook stands at the intersection of those disciplines, but its purpose is practical: to help people see their relationships more clearly and participate in them more intentionally.

I also acknowledge the couples, families, clients, students, colleagues, and communities whose experiences have reinforced a central truth: relationships are not strengthened by perfection. They are strengthened by awareness, courage, and the willingness to keep learning. Every relationship carries patterns. Every person carries stories. Every partnership faces stress. The question is whether those experiences become reasons to retreat or opportunities to understand the system more honestly.

To the readers who will use this workbook with care, I offer my respect. The decision to examine a relationship requires humility. The decision to practice repair requires courage. The decision to keep showing up with intentional action is an act of resilience. My hope is that this workbook gives you language, structure, and direction as you continue the work of building love that can learn.

TABLE OF CONTENTS

PREFACE

BEFORE THE WORK BEGINS

This workbook was created from a simple but demanding belief: relationships can learn. They can learn from stress, from conflict, from disappointment, from patterns that repeat, and from the quiet moments when two people finally become willing to ask a better question. Love is often described as something people fall into, find, lose, or recover, but long-term relationship resilience requires something more disciplined than emotion alone. It requires awareness, reflection, feedback, responsibility, repair, and the ability to adapt without losing the core commitment that brought two people together.

The Learning Relationship Workbook was designed as a practical companion to the larger relationship framework that applies business principles, cognitive psychology, behavioral science, and systems thinking to intimate partnership. In business, organizations that fail to learn become fragile. They repeat mistakes, ignore feedback, protect outdated assumptions, and mistake activity for progress. Relationships can suffer in the same way. A couple may remain busy, attached, committed, or emotionally invested while still repeating patterns that slowly weaken trust, closeness, and shared direction.

This workbook is not built on the idea that love should become corporate, mechanical, or transactional. It is built on the belief that love deserves structure because love matters. The language of systems, feedback loops, personal mastery, mental models, shared vision, team learning, and resilience gives couples a way to examine what is often felt but not clearly understood. It helps partners move from blame to pattern recognition, from reaction to reflection, from unspoken expectation to shared language, and from emotional survival to intentional growth.

The work ahead asks for honesty. Some exercises may feel simple, while others may uncover difficult truths. You may notice patterns you have avoided naming. You may recognize where you have waited for your partner to change while overlooking your own role in the system. You may discover that the relationship has strengths worth protecting and wounds that require more care than you expected. This is part of the process. A learning relationship does not grow by pretending everything is fine. It grows by becoming strong enough to tell the truth with responsibility.

This workbook can be used by individuals or couples. If you are using it alone, let the work begin with your own awareness. Do not use the exercises as a private courtroom against your partner. Use them to understand your role, your values, your assumptions, your needs, and your choices. If you are using it with your partner, move slowly and respectfully. The goal is not to complete pages. The goal is to create conversations that help the relationship become more conscious of itself.

This workbook is educational and reflective. It is not a replacement for therapy, counseling, crisis intervention, medical care, legal advice, or professional support. If your relationship involves abuse, coercive control, intimidation, threats, active addiction, ongoing betrayal, severe emotional harm, or concerns about safety, please seek qualified professional support. Reflection is powerful, but it should never be used as a substitute for protection.

The central idea of this workbook is that resilience is shaped through intentional action in the present moment. It is the choice to show up. It is the small step in the right direction when the old pattern is available. It is the pause before defense, the repair before resentment hardens, the question before assumption becomes certainty, and the commitment to keep learning even when love becomes difficult.

This workbook begins with the relationship as a system. It ends with the relationship as a continuing practice. The pages between are an invitation to study love with maturity, courage, and care.

INTRODUCTION

WHY RELATIONSHIPS NEED A LEARNING SYSTEM

Most people enter relationships with hope, attraction, affection, and some private image of what love is supposed to become. They may imagine stability, partnership, loyalty, family, emotional closeness, shared ambition, or simply the relief of being known by another person. These hopes are not naïve; they are deeply human. The difficulty is that hope alone does not teach two people how to build a relationship that can withstand pressure. Love may open the door, but it does not automatically create the system needed to sustain connection over time.

This workbook begins with a different assumption. A relationship is not only an emotional bond; it is a living system. It has patterns, habits, communication channels, decision rules, stress responses, unspoken expectations, shared routines, emotional histories, and repair mechanisms. Some of those parts are visible, while others operate quietly beneath the surface. When the system is healthy, the relationship can absorb stress, receive feedback, adjust behavior, and continue learning. When the system is strained, the same argument repeats, the same hurt resurfaces, and the same emotional distance returns, even when both people say they want things to improve.

In business, a struggling organization is rarely repaired by passion alone. A company may have talented people, a meaningful mission, and strong potential, but if its systems are disorganized, its feedback loops are broken, its leadership is reactive, or its teams are not learning from mistakes, the organization becomes vulnerable. The same is true in relationships. Two people may love each other and still be operating within a system that keeps producing disconnection. They may care deeply and still fail to listen effectively. They may want peace and still repeat conflict patterns that neither partner fully understands.

The purpose of this workbook is to help you see the relationship more clearly. It is designed for individuals and couples who want to repair, strengthen, and evolve an existing relationship by applying the principles of systems thinking, personal mastery, mental models, shared vision, and team learning. These ideas come from the language of organizational learning, but they translate with surprising relevance into intimate life. A relationship, like any living system, must learn if it is going to survive change.

This workbook is not asking you to treat love like a business transaction. It is not asking you to reduce your partner to a role, your emotions to data, or your relationship to a performance report. The goal is not to make love colder, more mechanical, or more corporate. The goal is to bring structure to what often becomes chaotic. Business principles are useful here because they provide a disciplined way to observe patterns, identify breakdowns, clarify expectations, strengthen communication, and make intentional adjustments before the relationship reaches a crisis point.

Many relationships suffer because people focus only on the visible problem. They argue about money, chores, sex, parenting, family boundaries, emotional distance, tone of voice, time, trust, or attention. These issues matter, but they are often symptoms of a deeper system. The question is not only, "What are we fighting about?" The deeper question is, "What pattern keeps bringing us back to this same place?" A learning relationship does not simply react to the latest conflict. It studies the pattern beneath the conflict.

This workbook will guide you through that process. You will begin by seeing the relationship as a system. You will examine recurring feedback loops and identify where communication breaks down. You will explore the mental models each partner brings into conflict, including assumptions about love, support, safety, independence, loyalty, and responsibility. You will then shift toward personal mastery, which means developing the ability to notice your own patterns, regulate your responses, and show up with greater intention inside the relationship.

From there, the workbook moves into shared vision and team learning. Many couples are working hard but not always working toward the same relationship. One person may be pursuing closeness, while the other is pursuing peace. One may define success as emotional transparency, while the other defines it as stability and reduced conflict. One may want growth, while the other may want predictability. Without shared vision, two people can be committed and still misaligned. The exercises in this workbook will help you clarify what you are building together.

Stress will also be treated as a major part of the relationship system. Every couple eventually faces pressure. Financial strain, career demands, health concerns, grief, parenting responsibilities, family conflict, relocation, aging, disappointment, and uncertainty all place weight on the relationship. The question is not whether stress will appear. The question is whether the relationship knows how to learn under stress. A learning relationship does not avoid pressure; it develops the capacity to respond to pressure with greater awareness, coordination, and repair.

One of the central beliefs of this workbook is that resilience is not a personality trait reserved for certain couples. Resilience is shaped through repeated choices. It is the choice to show up through intentional actions in the present moment. It is built through small steps in the right direction, especially when those steps are inconvenient, uncomfortable, or emotionally difficult. In relationships, resilience is not proven by never struggling. It is revealed in the willingness to pause, listen, repair, adjust, and return to the work of love with greater honesty.

This workbook is intended to be practical. You will not be asked only to read; you will be asked to reflect, write, discuss, notice, and practice. Some exercises may feel simple at first, but simplicity does not mean shallowness. The most important relational shifts often begin with basic acts that have been neglected: naming a pattern, listening without preparing a defense, asking a better question, clarifying an assumption, offering repair before resentment hardens, or choosing one small behavior that moves the relationship toward health.

You may use this workbook alone or with your partner. If you use it alone, approach the exercises as a way to understand your own role in the relationship system. The purpose is not to diagnose your partner from a distance or collect evidence against them. The purpose is to increase your awareness of the patterns you participate in and the choices available to you.

If you use it with your partner, move slowly. Do not rush through the exercises simply to complete them. The value of the workbook is not in finishing pages; it is in creating conversations that may not have happened otherwise.

It is also important to approach this work with emotional responsibility. A workbook can support reflection and growth, but it cannot replace professional help when the relationship involves abuse, coercion, untreated addiction, ongoing betrayal, severe emotional harm, threats, intimidation, or unresolved trauma. In those situations, safety and professional guidance matter more than completing exercises together. A learning relationship requires honesty, but it also requires safety. No person should be asked to use reflection as a substitute for protection.

As you move through this workbook, you will be invited to think like a systems observer, not a courtroom attorney. The goal is not to prove who is right. The goal is to understand what is happening. Blame often narrows attention. Curiosity expands it. When couples become trapped in blame, they usually study each other's failures. When they become capable of learning, they begin to study the system they have created together, including the parts they inherited, the parts they repeated, and the parts they now have the power to redesign.

This does not mean both partners are always equally responsible for every problem. They are not. Some harms are asymmetrical. Some behaviors require direct accountability. Some wounds cannot be softened by calling them "patterns." A learning relationship does not erase responsibility; it makes responsibility more precise. It asks each person to examine what they are doing, what they are avoiding, what they are protecting, and what they are willing to change.

The work ahead is not about becoming a perfect couple. It is about becoming a more aware one. It is about learning how to notice the system before it collapses into crisis. It is about replacing automatic reaction with intentional response. It is about creating a shared language for stress, repair, values, growth, and resilience. Most of all, it is about recognizing that love must keep learning if it is going to remain alive.

A relationship that learns can change direction. A relationship that learns can repair more honestly. A relationship that learns can make room for growth without treating growth as a threat. This workbook was created for those who are willing to examine love with maturity, courage, and care; not because the relationship is broken beyond repair, but because every lasting relationship must eventually decide whether it will repeat its patterns or learn from them.

HOW TO USE THIS WORKBOOK

A practical guide for pacing, reflection, discussion, and continued application.

This workbook was designed to be used slowly, honestly, and repeatedly. It is not meant to be rushed through in a weekend or completed like an assignment. The work of strengthening a relationship requires attention, not speed. A relationship system does not change simply because two people understand a concept. It changes when understanding becomes observation, observation becomes conversation, conversation becomes intentional action, and intentional action becomes a repeated practice.

You may use this workbook individually, with your partner, or alongside a counselor, therapist, coach, clergy member, or other trusted professional. Each approach has value. If you are using it alone, the purpose is to examine your own awareness, assumptions, reactions, and choices within the relationship system. It is not designed to help you build a private case against your partner. If you are using it together, the purpose is to create structured conversations that are more thoughtful than the conversations that usually happen in moments of stress. If you are using it with professional support, the exercises can help organize important themes and give language to patterns that may otherwise remain difficult to explain.

Before beginning, it is important to understand that this workbook is not a diagnostic tool. The assessments, reflections, and exercises are not designed to label you, label your partner, or determine the final condition of your relationship. A score, checklist, or written response can provide useful information, but it cannot capture the full complexity of a human bond. The purpose of the exercises is to create awareness. Awareness is the beginning of change, but it is not the same as judgment.

Some exercises will ask you to reflect privately before discussing your answers with your partner. This is intentional. Many couples move too quickly into debate before they have taken time to understand their own internal experience. Private reflection allows each person to slow down, identify assumptions, and clarify what they actually think and feel before entering conversation. When you do share your responses, do so with care. The goal is not to win the interpretation. The goal is to understand what each person is experiencing inside the same relationship system.

You may notice that some questions feel repetitive across chapters. This is also intentional. Relationships are patterned systems, and patterns rarely reveal themselves through a single question. The same theme may appear in different forms across communication, conflict, stress, support, repair, and shared vision. When something appears repeatedly, pay attention. Repetition often indicates an important feedback loop. It may show where the relationship is stuck, where one or both partners feel unheard, or where the system has learned to protect itself in ways that now create distance.

Move through the workbook in order if possible. The sections build on one another. Systems thinking comes first because it teaches you to look beyond isolated events. Feedback loops come next because relationships depend on the ability to receive and respond to information. Mental models follow because conflict is shaped not only by what happens, but by the meaning each person assigns to what happens. Personal mastery then asks each partner to examine their own role in the system. Shared vision creates direction. Team learning helps the relationship function during stress. Relationship review meetings turn learning into a repeated practice. Long-term resilience brings the process together into a sustainable plan.

Although the chapters are arranged in a sequence, you may return to earlier sections at any time. In fact, you should. A workbook like this becomes more useful when revisited after new conversations, conflicts, decisions, or seasons of stress. A couple may complete the system map early in the process and then return to it months later with a much deeper understanding. An exercise that seems simple at first may become more meaningful after the relationship has practiced more honest feedback. Learning is not linear. It often moves in cycles.

When completing written exercises, answer with enough detail to make your responses useful. One-word answers may be easy, but they rarely create insight. At the same time, do not pressure yourself to write perfectly. This is not an academic paper, a legal statement, or a performance. Your written responses are tools for reflection. Write in the language that helps you tell the truth clearly. The more honest the response, the more useful the exercise becomes.

When discussing exercises as a couple, choose timing carefully. Do not begin a difficult chapter in the middle of an argument, late at night when both people are exhausted, or immediately after a painful event when neither person has the capacity to listen well. A learning conversation requires emotional availability. You do not need ideal conditions, but you do need enough steadiness to remain respectful. If the conversation becomes flooded, defensive, or harmful, pause. A pause is not a failure. Sometimes the most mature choice is to stop before the system repeats its old pattern.

It may help to set a regular time for workbook conversations. Some couples may choose one chapter per week. Others may choose one exercise every few days. Some may need more time because the material touches long-standing pain. There is no single correct pace. What matters is that the work remains intentional and sustainable. The goal is not to finish quickly. The goal is to create a relationship practice that can continue after the workbook is complete.

As you work through the exercises, you will encounter moments where you feel defensive. This is normal. Reflection can be uncomfortable because it asks you to see not only what has been done to you, but also how you respond, protect, withdraw, pursue, criticize, avoid, assume, or repeat. Defensiveness should not be treated as proof that the exercise is wrong. It may be a signal that the exercise has touched something important. When defensiveness appears, slow down. Ask what you are protecting. Ask what feels threatened. Ask whether the reaction is connected only to the present moment or also to a longer history.

You may also encounter grief. Some people discover that their relationship has been operating without shared vision for years. Some realize that repeated conflict has taught them to expect disappointment. Some recognize that they stopped asking for support because the system trained them to expect dismissal. These discoveries can be painful. They can also become turning points. Naming a pattern does not automatically repair it, but unnamed patterns often control the relationship from beneath the surface.

When the workbook asks you to identify your own role in a pattern, it is not asking you to accept responsibility for another person's harmful behavior. This distinction matters. Personal mastery is not self-blame. It is the disciplined practice of knowing yourself clearly enough to choose your response with intention. If your partner has harmed you, accountability belongs where it belongs. If you have harmed your partner, accountability belongs with you. Systems thinking helps reveal interaction patterns, but it should never be used to minimize abuse, coercion, manipulation, intimidation, or betrayal.

If you and your partner disagree during the exercises, try to resist the immediate urge to correct each other's memory. In many relationship conflicts, the facts matter, but the emotional meaning attached to the facts also matters. Two people can remember the same event differently because each person experienced the event through a different mental model, emotional state, and history of expectations. This does not mean every interpretation is equally accurate. It means that learning begins when both people become curious about how the other person made sense of the experience.

A useful phrase throughout this workbook is, "Help me understand how you experienced that." This question does not require you to surrender your own perspective. It simply opens space for another one. In a relationship system, understanding is not agreement. You can understand why something hurt your partner without agreeing with every conclusion they drew. You can understand why your partner became defensive without excusing the behavior that followed. You can understand the system more clearly without abandoning your own truth.

Some exercises will ask you to create agreements. Keep those agreements small enough to practice. Couples often fail at change because they make promises that are too broad, too emotional, or too vague. "We will communicate better" is not an agreement. It is a wish. "On Sunday evenings, we will spend twenty minutes reviewing stress points for the upcoming week without problem-solving until both people have spoken" is an agreement. A learning relationship depends on specific, observable actions that can be practiced, reviewed, and adjusted.

As you proceed, pay attention to the difference between insight and implementation. Insight is the moment you realize something important. Implementation is what you do differently after the realization. Many couples have powerful conversations and then return to the same habits because the system has not been redesigned. This workbook will repeatedly ask you to translate insight into action. The action does not need to be dramatic. Often the most important changes are small, repeated, and visible.

You may find it helpful to keep a separate notebook or digital document for longer reflections. The pages of this workbook may guide the process, but your relationship history will likely require more space than a worksheet can provide. Record patterns, agreements, questions, and moments of repair. Over time, these notes can become evidence that the relationship is learning. They may also show where the same issues remain unresolved and require deeper attention.

If a chapter feels too difficult to complete together, complete it separately first. Then decide whether to discuss the entire exercise or only one part. Not every reflection needs to become a full conversation immediately. Some material requires time. Some truths need to be approached carefully. The measure of progress is not how much is disclosed at once, but whether the relationship is moving toward greater honesty, safety, and responsibility.

This workbook should be used with compassion, but not avoidance. Compassion without honesty becomes denial. Honesty without compassion becomes injury. The work requires both. You are being asked to tell the truth in a way that supports learning rather than punishment. You are being asked to listen in a way that supports understanding rather than defense. You are being asked to notice the relationship system with enough courage to admit what is not working and enough hope to practice what could work better.

At the end of each chapter, pause before moving forward. Ask yourself what you learned, what surprised you, what felt difficult, and what small step should come next. The next step matters because resilience is shaped through action in the present moment. You do not need to repair the entire relationship at once. You need to begin creating conditions where repair is possible. One honest conversation, one clearer agreement, one softer response, one interrupted pattern, one act of accountability, one moment of shared courage; these are the small movements through which a relationship begins to learn.

The workbook will not do the work for you. It will provide structure, language, and direction. The deeper work will happen in the pauses, the conversations, the discomfort, the decisions, and the repeated choice to show up with intention. A learning relationship is not one that has solved every problem. It is one that refuses to stop learning from the problems it faces.

THE RELATIONSHIP IS THE SYSTEM

THIS CHAPTER FOCUSES ON OBSERVING, MAPPING, AND STRENGTHENING RELATIONAL PATTERNS

CHAPTER FOCUS

This chapter helps you move from blame to pattern recognition. You will examine the relationship as a living system shaped by communication, stress, repair, expectations, emotional history, and repeated choices.

CHAPTER 1

THE RELATIONSHIP IS THE SYSTEM

Seeing the relationship as an interconnected system of patterns, pressures, strengths, and repeated responses.

Most relationship problems are discussed as if they belong to one person. One partner is described as distant, emotional, defensive, irresponsible, controlling, avoidant, critical, needy, careless, or difficult. These descriptions may contain pieces of truth, but they are rarely complete enough to explain what is happening inside the relationship. A relationship is not simply one person's behavior placed beside another person's reaction. It is a system of repeated exchanges, emotional signals, learned expectations, protective strategies, unmet needs, external pressures, and attempts at repair. This systems view is consistent with family systems theory, which understands relational functioning as an interconnected emotional process rather than a set of isolated individual behaviors (Bowen, 1978; Stanton, 2012). When two people live inside the same relationship long enough, they do not merely respond to each other; they begin to organize around each other.

Systems thinking begins by shifting the question. Instead of asking only, "What is wrong with my partner?" or "Why do I keep reacting this way?" it asks, "What pattern are we participating in?" This shift reflects the broader discipline of systems thinking, which focuses attention on recurring patterns, interdependence, and the structures that produce repeated outcomes over time (Senge, 2006). This does not remove personal responsibility. It sharpens it. A system is not an excuse for harmful behavior, nor is it a way to soften accountability when one person has caused real damage. Systems thinking simply recognizes that relationship patterns are often maintained by more than one action, more than one moment, and more than one interpretation.

Every relationship has a design, even when no one designed it intentionally. The design may include how decisions are made, how conflict begins, how apologies happen, how stress is handled, how silence is interpreted, how affection is expressed, how money is discussed, how extended family enters the relationship, how disappointment is managed, and how each partner signals emotional need. Some couples develop a design that supports openness and repair. Others develop a design that protects the relationship from immediate discomfort but slowly weakens trust. Avoiding hard conversations may create temporary peace, but over time it can teach the system that honesty is unsafe. Explosive conflict may create temporary release, but over time it can teach both partners that closeness comes with emotional danger.

To see the relationship as a system, you must learn to look beyond the surface event. The surface event may be a disagreement about spending, a forgotten task, a sharp tone, a missed call, a lack of intimacy, or a parenting decision. Beneath that event is often a familiar sequence. One partner notices something and interprets it through a personal history. The body reacts before the mind fully explains why. A tone changes. A facial expression hardens. One partner pursues; the other withdraws. One criticizes; the other defends. One becomes quieter, the other becomes louder. By the end of the exchange, the couple may be arguing about the original issue, but the emotional system is now responding to something much larger: disrespect, abandonment, inadequacy, control, rejection, invisibility, or fear.

A relationship system is shaped by inputs. These inputs include sleep, work stress, financial strain, health problems, parenting demands, grief, cultural expectations, family history, unresolved injuries, time together, time apart, emotional capacity, and the quality of recent repair. Stress theories, including Conservation of Resources theory, suggest that people are affected not only by the stressor itself, but by threats to valued resources such as time, energy, stability, emotional support, and relational security (Hobfoll, 1989). When these inputs change, the system changes. Systems thinking helps couples stop treating every conflict as a separate mystery. It asks them to examine what conditions make the relationship more reactive, more distant, more generous, or more capable of learning.

In business, leaders often examine systems when outcomes become inconsistent or harmful. If a company repeatedly misses deadlines, the solution is not always to accuse one employee of laziness. The organization may need to examine workflow, communication, incentives, training, role clarity, resource limitations, leadership decisions, and feedback channels. This reflects the logic of organizational learning, where recurring problems are examined as products of larger systems rather than merely individual failures (Argyris & Schön, 1978; Senge, 2006). The same principle applies to relationships. If a couple repeatedly collapses into the same conflict, the problem may not be only the topic being discussed. The relationship may lack a reliable process for handling disagreement, emotional safety, shared language, recovery practices, or a clear way to move from hurt to repair.

A system can become loyal to dysfunction because dysfunction is familiar. This is one reason relationships can repeat patterns that both partners dislike. A couple may say they want better communication, yet the system may be organized around avoidance because avoidance has prevented immediate conflict in the past. Another couple may say they want closeness, yet the system may be organized around criticism and defense because criticism has become the only way one partner signals distress and defense has become the only way the other partner protects self-worth. The pattern continues not because it works well, but because it has become the practiced route.

When couples begin to examine the relationship as a system, they often discover that the issue is not simply a lack of love. They may love each other and still have poor feedback loops. They may be committed and still have competing mental models. They may want the same future but lack shared language for building it. They may value each other deeply and still harm each other through automatic responses. Systems thinking makes room for this complexity. It allows a couple to say, "We are not enemies, but the pattern we are in is hurting us."

This shift matters because many couples' waste energy trying to prove who started the problem. The starting point may matter in some situations, especially when harm has occurred, but repeated relational patterns usually become circular. One partner withdraws because they feel criticized. The other criticizes because they feel abandoned by the withdrawal. The withdrawal confirms the fear of abandonment, while the criticism confirms the fear of failure or attack. This type of circular pattern is central to systemic approaches to couple and family functioning, where each person's behavior becomes both a response to and a trigger for the other person's behavior (Bowen, 1978; Stanton, 2012). Systems thinking interrupts this narrow view by asking each partner to study the loop.

The first step in studying the loop is slowing down enough to identify what usually happens. Most couples know the topic of their recurring arguments, but they do not always know the sequence. They know they fight about money, but not the exact emotional chain that turns budgeting into accusation. They know they argue about intimacy, but not the hidden meanings each partner attaches to rejection, pressure, desirability, safety, or emotional closeness. They know they disagree about family boundaries, but not how loyalty, guilt, obligation, and identity enter the conversation. Systems thinking asks for more than the topic. It asks for the pattern.

Seeing the relationship as a system also means recognizing that the relationship has strengths. Systems thinking is not only a search for dysfunction. It is also a search for what already works. Every couple has moments when the system functions better. Relationship maintenance research suggests that positive behaviors, openness, assurances, shared tasks, and other maintenance practices are associated with healthier relational functioning (Ogolsky & Bowers, 2013). These strengths are not accidental. They are part of the system too, and they can be studied, protected, and expanded.

The purpose of the exercises in this chapter is to help you begin mapping your relationship system. Mapping does not solve everything, but it gives you a clearer view of the terrain. A couple cannot redesign a pattern they have not identified. They cannot repair a feedback loop they cannot see. They cannot create shared vision if they do not understand the system they are currently living inside. The work begins with observation because observation gives the relationship a chance to become conscious of itself.

RELATIONSHIP SYSTEM MAP

EXERCISE 1.1

Before You Begin
Complete this first individually. If you are working with a partner, share only after both people have had time to reflect privately.

Prompt	Reflection Space
What is currently working in this part of the relationship?	
What feels strained, unclear, or repeatedly difficult?	
What pattern do we tend to repeat in this area?	
What does each partner seem to need in this area?	
What do I personally contribute to the strength or weakness of this area?	
What would improvement look like in observable behavior?	
Our relationship system currently tends to:	
We want our relationship system to learn how to:	

THE REPEATING PATTERN

EXERCISE 1.2

Before You Begin
Choose one recurring conflict or tension in the relationship. Begin with a pattern that is meaningful but manageable.

Prompt	Reflection Space
The issue we keep returning to is:	
What usually happens first?	
How do I interpret it?	
How does my body react?	
What do I usually say or do next?	
How does my partner usually respond?	
How does the conflict usually end?	
What remains unresolved?	
Our repeating pattern can be described without blame this way:	

INPUTS THAT AFFECT THE RELATIONSHIP

EXERCISE 1.3

Before You Begin
Relationships do not operate in isolation. Identify the external and internal pressures that influence how the relationship functions.

Prompt	Reflection Space
Which input is currently placing the most pressure on the relationship?	
Which input are we underestimating?	
Which input has improved recently?	
Which input could we adjust with intentional action?	
What is one small change that could reduce unnecessary pressure on the system?	

STRENGTHS IN THE SYSTEM

EXERCISE 1.4

Before You Begin
A relationship system is not only its problems. Identify what the relationship already does well.

Prompt	Reflection Space
When do we function best as a couple?	
What helps us feel connected?	
What kind of stress have we handled well in the past?	
What does my partner do that strengthens the relationship?	
What do I do that strengthens the relationship?	
One sign that our relationship is capable of learning is:	

FROM BLAME TO PATTERN RECOGNITION

EXERCISE 1.5

Before You Begin
Rewrite blame statements through a systems lens. The goal is to describe the issue as a pattern rather than only as a personal failure.

Prompt	Reflection Space
I usually think the problem is:	
A broader pattern I can observe is:	
I get frustrated because my partner:	
When this happens, our system tends to:	
The role I often take in the pattern is:	
What changes when I describe the issue as a pattern rather than only as a personal failure?	

CHAPTER REFLECTION

EXERCISE 1.6

Before You Begin
Use this space before moving forward. The goal is not to solve every issue immediately; the goal is to see the relationship with greater clarity.

Prompt	Reflection Space
What did I learn about our relationship system?	
What pattern became clearer to me?	
What did I notice about my own role in the system?	
What strength did I identify that I do not want to overlook?	
What issue needs careful attention in future chapters?	
What is one small action I can take this week to help the relationship system function better?	

CHAPTER COMMITMENT

EXERCISE 1.7

Before You Begin
A learning relationship begins when at least one person becomes willing to observe the system honestly.

Prompt	Reflection Space
My small intentional action this week will be:	
I will know I practiced it when:	
I will review this commitment on:	

CONCLUSION

A relationship becomes more workable when it can be seen as a system rather than a series of isolated disappointments. This does not make responsibility disappear. It makes responsibility more accurate. Once partners can identify the pattern, they can stop spending all of their energy reacting to the latest symptom and begin studying the structure that keeps producing it.

The work of this chapter is foundational because systems thinking changes the way couples locate the problem. Instead of treating one partner as the entire source of distress, the couple begins to ask what the relationship has learned to do under pressure. This shift creates room for accountability, curiosity, and redesign. It also prepares the couple to examine the places where the system receives information but fails to respond.

The next chapter moves into those information pathways. Every relationship produces feedback through words, silence, distance, emotion, repeated complaints, and unmet needs. When those signals are ignored, punished, or misunderstood, the relationship stops learning from itself. Chapter 2 will help you identify broken feedback loops and begin redesigning the way the relationship listens.

WHEN THE SYSTEM STOPS LISTENING

IDENTIFYING BROKEN FEEDBACK LOOPS AND REDESIGNING HOW THE RELATIONSHIP RECEIVES, INTERPRETS, AND RESPONDS TO IMPORTANT SIGNALS.

CHAPTER FOCUS

This chapter helps you identify broken feedback loops and redesign how the relationship receives, interprets, and responds to important signals.

CHAPTER 2

WHEN THE SYSTEM STOPS LISTENING

Identifying broken feedback loops and redesigning how the relationship receives, interprets, and responds to important signals.

Every relationship has feedback. Some feedback is spoken directly, some is communicated through tone, distance, facial expression, repeated complaint, silence, irritability, affection, withdrawal, generosity, or the absence of something that used to be present. Feedback is the information a relationship produces about how it is functioning. In organizational learning, feedback is essential because it allows a system to detect error, respond to changing conditions, and adjust behavior over time (Argyris & Schön, 1978; Senge, 2006). A relationship does not become unhealthy because feedback exists. It becomes unhealthy when feedback is ignored, punished, distorted, delayed, or repeated so often without response that one or both partners stop believing the system can learn.

In business, feedback loops are essential to organizational survival. A company that cannot hear from its customers, employees, financial reports, or internal processes will eventually make decisions based on assumptions rather than reality. When feedback is functioning well, the organization can notice problems early and adjust before small inefficiencies become major failures. This is consistent with learning organization theory, which emphasizes the need for systems to receive, interpret, and respond to information in order to adapt (Senge, 2006). Relationships work in a similar way. A partner may raise a concern gently at first. If it is dismissed, minimized, mocked, or turned back against them, the concern does not disappear. It usually returns with more force, more pain, or more distance.

A feedback loop is the pathway through which information travels, produces a response, and influences future behavior. In a healthy relationship, one partner can say, "I am feeling disconnected," and the relationship has enough safety to receive that information. Although psychological safety was originally studied in work teams, the concept is useful here because learning requires an environment where people can take interpersonal risks, speak honestly, and raise concerns without fear of humiliation or punishment (Edmondson, 1999). The loop is not healthy because feedback is always comfortable. It is healthy because feedback can move through the system without being destroyed.

When a feedback loop is broken, the relationship stops learning from its own signals. One partner may speak, but the other hears criticism. One partner may ask for closeness, but the other hears control. One partner may express pain, but the other hears accusation. One partner may become quiet, but the other interprets the silence as punishment rather than overwhelm. Over time, the relationship becomes less responsive to reality and more responsive to defensiveness, fear, history, and assumption. The system continues to produce information, but the information no longer leads to useful adjustment.

Many couples do not recognize broken feedback loops because they are focused on the content of the disagreement. They remember what was said, but not how the message moved through the system. A partner says, "I need more help," and the conversation becomes an argument about whether the other person does enough. A partner says, "I miss you," and the conversation becomes a defense of work hours, fatigue, or responsibilities. A partner says, "That hurt me," and the conversation becomes a debate about intention. The original feedback may have been simple: something needs attention. But the system transforms the message into threat.

This transformation is one of the most important things to understand about relational learning. Feedback often fails not because the message is unimportant, but because the relationship does not have a safe process for receiving it. In organizational learning, defensive routines can prevent people from examining the very assumptions and behaviors that need to change (Argyris, 1977; Argyris & Schön, 1978). If feedback has historically led to conflict, shame, rejection, or emotional overload, both partners may begin to protect themselves from it. The speaker may delay speaking until resentment builds. The listener may prepare a defense before the message is complete. By the time the feedback is spoken, the nervous system is no longer listening for information; it is preparing for danger.

A learning relationship must become more skilled at distinguishing feedback from attack. This does not mean every complaint is delivered well. Some feedback is harsh, careless, exaggerated, or poorly timed. Some concerns arrive wrapped in accusation because they have been ignored for too long. Some partners use feedback as a disguise for criticism or control. For this reason, both sides of the loop matter. The person giving feedback has a responsibility to communicate as clearly and respectfully as possible. The person receiving feedback has a responsibility to listen for the information beneath the discomfort.

Broken feedback loops often begin with small missed signals. A partner stops initiating affection. A recurring joke becomes sharper. A routine conversation becomes shorter. One person begins staying busy to avoid emotional contact. Another begins asking the same question repeatedly, hoping for a different answer. The relationship may not be in crisis yet, but the system is producing data. If the couple notices these signals early, they can intervene with care. If they ignore them, the signals may intensify until they become conflict, distance, or emotional exhaustion.

Some couples develop feedback fatigue. They have talked about the same issue so many times that both people assume nothing new can be learned. One partner thinks, "I have already said this." The other thinks, "I have already heard this." The relationship becomes numb to the repeated signal. This is dangerous because repetition often means the issue has not been integrated into the system. Hearing means the words reached your ears. Integrating means the information influenced awareness, behavior, or agreement.

This is where the distinction between surface correction and deeper learning becomes useful. Sometimes a couple makes a small adjustment to stop the immediate discomfort. One partner apologizes quickly. The other accepts it quickly. The conflict ends, but the underlying pattern remains untouched. This resembles the distinction between single-loop learning, which corrects immediate errors, and double-loop learning, which questions the underlying assumptions and governing patterns that keep producing the error (Argyris & Schön, 1978). Deeper learning asks why the issue keeps returning and what the relationship needs to learn so the pattern does not regenerate itself.

A learning relationship needs a feedback process that is clear enough to be useful and safe enough to be repeated. Communication matters, but relationship research also suggests that communication and satisfaction influence each other in complex ways over time, meaning couples should avoid assuming that one better conversation alone will automatically repair a deeper pattern (Johnson et al., 2021). Structured relationship education and relationship-focused programs have been associated with improvements in couple satisfaction and communication, though outcomes vary depending on the quality of the program, the couple's needs, and the way the practices are implemented (Javadivala et al., 2021).

A strong feedback loop has several qualities. It allows concerns to be raised before they become emergencies. It allows both partners to clarify meaning. It separates impact from intention without dismissing either. It turns repeated complaints into specific requests. It creates follow-up so the same issue does not vanish after one emotional conversation. It makes repair normal rather than humiliating. It treats feedback as information for the relationship system, not as a weapon against one person's character.

FEEDBACK LOOP AUDIT

EXERCISE 2.1

Before You Begin
Think about the last three times one partner raised a concern in the relationship. Notice whether the concern produced understanding, decision, repair, or change.

Prompt	Reflection Space
Concern one: What was raised, how was it communicated, and how did the other person respond?	
Concern two: What was raised, how was it communicated, and how did the other person respond?	
Concern three: What was raised, how was it communicated, and how did the other person respond?	
When feedback is raised in our relationship, the system usually:	
The most common reason feedback does not lead to change is:	
One thing our feedback loop needs to learn is:	

WHAT I SAY VERSUS WHAT YOU HEAR

EXERCISE 2.2

Before You Begin
Many feedback loops break because the message sent is not the same as the message received. Separate words, meaning, interpretation, and emotional impact.

Prompt	Reflection Space
The statement or concern is:	
When I say this, what I am trying to communicate is:	
When I say this, what I am afraid my partner hears is:	
When my partner hears this, they may interpret it as:	
The request I need to make more clearly is:	
A question I could ask before reacting is:	

MISSED SIGNALS INVENTORY

EXERCISE 2.3

Before You Begin
Feedback does not always begin as a direct statement. Sometimes the system sends signals before the issue becomes a conflict.

Prompt	Reflection Space
Which signal appears most often?	
Which signal do I tend to ignore?	
Which signal does my partner seem to ignore?	
Which signal usually appears before conflict?	
What might this signal be trying to tell the relationship?	
What would it look like to respond to this signal earlier and with more care?	

DEFENSIVE ROUTINE REFLECTION

EXERCISE 2.4

Before You Begin
Defensiveness is one of the most common reasons feedback loops break. Identify your defensive routines without using them as a source of shame.

Prompt	Reflection Space
The type of feedback that makes me most defensive is:	
I think I become defensive because:	
Underneath my defensiveness, I may be feeling:	
The cost of my defensiveness is:	
A more useful response would be:	
My practice sentence will be:	

FROM COMPLAINT TO CLEAR REQUEST

EXERCISE 2.5

Before You Begin
Repeated complaints often contain important feedback, but the relationship may not know how to translate them into clear requests.

Prompt	Reflection Space
The complaint is:	
The deeper concern underneath this complaint is:	
The emotional need underneath this concern is:	
The specific behavior that would help is:	
The request I can make is:	
For the next week, we will practice this specific behavior:	

FEEDBACK REPAIR CONVERSATION

EXERCISE 2.6

Before You Begin
Choose one issue that matters but is safe enough to discuss. Speak slowly and listen for information before defending.

Prompt	Reflection Space
Partner A: The feedback I have been trying to give is:	
Partner A: What I need you to understand is:	
Partner B: What I heard you say is:	
Partner B: One thing I can take responsibility for is:	
Shared reflection: What helped the conversation stay open?	
Shared agreement: What is one small adjustment we both agree to practice?	

CHAPTER REFLECTION

EXERCISE 2.7

Before You Begin
Reflect on how feedback currently functions in your relationship. The purpose is not perfect communication; the purpose is to make the relationship more capable of learning.

Prompt	Reflection Space
What did I learn about how feedback moves through our relationship?	
What kind of feedback do I avoid giving?	
What kind of feedback is hardest for me to receive?	
What signal have I been ignoring?	
What defensive routine do I need to become more aware of?	
What is one feedback loop that needs repair?	

CHAPTER COMMITMENT

EXERCISE 2.8

Before You Begin
A learning relationship does not ignore its own signals. This week, practice treating feedback as information before treating it as threat.

Prompt	Reflection Space
My small intentional action this week will be:	
I will know I practiced it when:	
One feedback signal I will pay closer attention to is:	
One defensive response I will work to interrupt is:	
I will review this commitment on:	

CONCLUSION

A relationship begins to change when it can listen to itself. Feedback is one of the ways the relationship speaks. Sometimes it speaks through direct words. Sometimes it speaks through distance, repeated conflict, emotional fatigue, silence, irritability, or the quiet absence of connection. When couples learn to hear these signals earlier and with less defensiveness, they create the conditions for repair before the system reaches crisis.

A stronger relationship does not require both people to speak perfectly. It requires both people to become more committed to understanding what the system is trying to reveal. The goal is not to remove discomfort from the relationship. The goal is to make discomfort useful. When feedback becomes safer, clearer, and more specific, the relationship gains the ability to adjust. It can notice strain before resentment hardens. It can name hurt before distance becomes normal. It can turn repeated complaints into shared responsibility.

The next chapter moves deeper into the meaning beneath conflict. Feedback loops often break because partners are not only responding to what was said; they are responding to the stories, assumptions, fears, and interpretations they carry into the moment. These internal frameworks are called mental models. To understand why the same feedback can sound like a request to one person and an attack to another, we must examine the stories each partner brings into love.

THE STORIES WE BRING INTO LOVE

UNDERSTANDING MENTAL MODELS, INHERITED BELIEFS, AND ASSUMPTIONS THAT SHAPE CONFLICT, REPAIR, AND EMOTIONAL INTERPRETATION.

CHAPTER FOCUS

This chapter helps you understand mental models, inherited beliefs, and assumptions that shape conflict, repair, and emotional interpretation.

CHAPTER 3

THE STORIES WE BRING INTO LOVE

Understanding mental models, inherited beliefs, and assumptions that shape conflict, repair, and emotional interpretation.

Conflict is rarely only about the moment in front of us. A disagreement may begin with a sentence, a look, a delay, a forgotten task, a change in tone, or an unmet expectation, but the meaning of that moment is shaped by much more than the event itself. Each partner enters the relationship carrying internal stories about love, safety, trust, loyalty, vulnerability, independence, responsibility, and rejection. These stories are often invisible until conflict activates them. When they are activated, two people may believe they are responding to each other, when in reality they are also responding to the meanings their minds have attached to what is happening.

In organizational learning, these internal stories are often called mental models. A mental model is a deeply held assumption, belief, interpretation, or expectation that shapes how a person understands reality. Senge described mental models as one of the core disciplines of a learning organization because they influence how people interpret events, define problems, and decide what actions are possible (Senge, 2006). In a relationship, mental models influence how partners interpret affection, silence, criticism, stress, distance, apology, conflict, and support. They become the lenses through which love is understood.

Mental models are powerful because they often feel like truth. A person may not think, "I am interpreting this through a learned belief." They may simply think, "This is what is happening." Cognitive approaches to therapy emphasize that automatic thoughts, assumptions, and interpretations can strongly shape emotional and behavioral responses (Beck, 2021). One partner may hear a request for help and interpret it as evidence that they are failing. Another may hear a request for space and interpret it as rejection. One may hear a suggestion and experience it as control. Another may hear silence and experience it as abandonment.

This is one reason couples can argue with such intensity about events that seem minor from the outside. The argument is not only about the dishes, the phone, the text message, the budget, the family visit, the tone of voice, or the forgotten errand. Cognitive-behavioral approaches to couple relationships suggest that relationship distress is often shaped by the meanings partners attach to each other's behavior, including assumptions, expectations, attributions, and emotional interpretations (Epstein & Baucom, 2002). To one person, the forgotten errand means, "I cannot rely on you." To the other, the frustration about the errand means, "Nothing I do is ever enough."

Mental models are shaped by experience. Family history, culture, childhood attachment, previous relationships, betrayal, disappointment, social expectations, religious values, gender roles, trauma, success, failure, and personal temperament all influence what a person expects from love. Attachment theory suggests that early relational experiences can shape expectations about safety, closeness, separation, and emotional responsiveness in later relationships (Bowlby, 1969; Hazan & Shaver, 1987). These patterns do not make a person broken. Adult attachment research has linked attachment patterns with relationship functioning and satisfaction, though these associations should be understood as patterns of influence rather than fixed relationship destinies (Candel & Turliuc, 2019; Hazan & Shaver, 1987).

A learning relationship must become willing to examine its mental models. This requires more than asking, "What happened?" It requires asking, "What did I make it mean?" That question is simple, but it can change the direction of a conflict. It separates the event from the interpretation. It allows a person to notice that the mind may have added meaning based on old pain, fear, habit, or expectation. This does not mean the interpretation is always wrong. Sometimes the meaning attached to an event is accurate. But it must be examined before it is treated as fact.

Many couples do not fight because they lack love. They fight because they are using different rulebooks. Each partner assumes the other understands the rules, then becomes hurt or frustrated when the rules are not followed. This is consistent with cognitive-behavioral couple frameworks, which emphasize that expectations, standards, assumptions, and attributions influence how partners interpret one another's behavior (Epstein & Baucom, 2002). The difficulty is that these rules were often never written, discussed, or agreed upon. They were inherited, absorbed, protected, or created in response to earlier experiences.

One person may believe love means constant emotional sharing. Another may believe love means loyalty, provision, and stability. These differences matter because love itself can be understood as involving multiple dimensions, including intimacy, passion, and commitment, which partners may value or express differently across the life of the relationship (Sternberg, 1986). One may believe conflict should be addressed immediately. Another may believe healthy people calm down first and speak later. One may believe independence protects the relationship. Another may believe independence signals emotional distance. These differences do not automatically mean one partner is wrong. They mean the couple may be operating from different internal definitions of love.

Mental models become especially important during conflict because the mind naturally tries to explain threat quickly. When a partner feels hurt, the brain often searches for a story that makes the hurt understandable. The story may be, "They do not care." "They are trying to control me." "I am not important." "I am being used." "I will be abandoned." "I cannot make mistakes here." Once the story forms, the body responds to the story as if it is reality. The partner may become angry, shut down, plead, criticize, overexplain, or withdraw, not only because of the present event, but because of the story activated by the event.

A learning relationship does not ask partners to abandon their stories immediately. Some stories formed for good reasons. They may have helped a person survive emotionally, maintain dignity, avoid harm, or make sense of difficult experiences. The goal is not to shame the story. The goal is to examine whether the story still serves the relationship. A mental model that once protected a person may later prevent intimacy. A belief that helped someone avoid being controlled may later make partnership feel threatening. A belief that helped someone become self-reliant may later make receiving support feel uncomfortable.

A key part of this chapter is learning to test assumptions. Assumption testing does not mean doubting every feeling. Feelings provide important information, but feelings are not always complete interpretations of reality. Cognitive-behavioral approaches often help individuals identify automatic thoughts, evaluate evidence, and consider alternative interpretations before reacting (Beck, 2021). A person can feel rejected without the partner intending rejection. A person can feel controlled when the partner is actually asking for collaboration. A person can feel criticized when the partner is expressing loneliness. Assumption testing creates a pause between interpretation and reaction.

The exercises in this chapter will help you identify some of the mental models operating inside your relationship. You will examine the stories you bring into conflict, the assumptions you make about your partner, the inherited beliefs that shape your expectations, and the interpretations that may turn feedback into threat. The purpose is not to prove that your interpretation is wrong. The purpose is to make interpretation visible. Once a mental model becomes visible, it can be discussed. Once it can be discussed, it can be tested. Once it can be tested, it can be revised. This is how a relationship begins to move from reaction to understanding.

MENTAL MODEL INVENTORY

EXERCISE 3.1

Before You Begin

Identify beliefs and assumptions that shape how you experience the relationship. Complete this individually before discussing it with your partner.

Prompt	Reflection Space
Love means:	
Commitment means:	
Trust means:	
Respect means:	
Support means:	
Conflict means:	
Apology means:	
Forgiveness means:	
If my partner really loved me, they would:	
One mental model I need to examine more carefully is:	

WHAT HAPPENED VERSUS WHAT I MADE IT MEAN

EXERCISE 3.2

Before You Begin
Choose a recent moment of conflict, distance, disappointment, or misunderstanding. Separate the event from the meaning attached to it.

Prompt	Reflection Space
What happened?	
What did I feel?	
What did I make it mean?	
What did I assume about my partner's intention?	
What evidence supported my interpretation?	
What evidence did not fully support my interpretation?	
What else could this have meant?	
A clearer request or response would have been:	

THE OLD STORY AND THE PRESENT MOMENT

EXERCISE 3.3

Before You Begin
Sometimes a present conflict activates an older story. Identify whether your reaction is connected only to the present moment or also to a longer history.

Prompt	Reflection Space
The reaction I often have is:	
The story that appears in my mind is:	
This story may be connected to:	
What did this old story once help me protect?	
How might this story be limiting the relationship now?	
What do I need to take responsibility for when this story is activated?	

ASSUMPTION TESTING PRACTICE

EXERCISE 3.4

Before You Begin
Assumptions often appear quickly in conflict. Slow down and test them before treating them as facts.

Prompt	Reflection Space
My assumption was:	
The situation that triggered it was:	
The evidence I had was:	
The evidence I did not have was:	
Another possible explanation is:	
A respectful question I could ask is:	
One assumption I will practice testing before reacting is:	

INHERITED RULEBOOK REFLECTION

EXERCISE 3.5

Before You Begin
Every person learns rules about relationships before entering a serious partnership. Identify the rulebook you may have inherited.

Prompt	Reflection Space
Growing up, I learned that conflict was:	
Growing up, I learned that affection was:	
Growing up, I learned that apology was:	
Growing up, I learned that emotions were:	
Growing up, I learned that loyalty meant:	
Which inherited rule still helps me?	
Which inherited rule harms or limits the relationship?	
A rule I want to intentionally build is:	

REWRITING A MENTAL MODEL

EXERCISE 3.6

Before You Begin
Choose one mental model that may be creating unnecessary conflict, distance, or defensiveness. Revise it into a more flexible model.

Prompt	Reflection Space
Current mental model:	
Where I may have learned this:	
How this model protects me:	
How this model harms me:	
How this model affects my partner:	
A more flexible mental model would be:	
A behavior that would support this new model is:	
Small action I will practice:	

MENTAL MODELS CONVERSATION

EXERCISE 3.7

Before You Begin
This exercise is designed for couples. Choose one belief or assumption each partner wants the other to understand. Speak slowly and listen without correcting immediately.

Prompt	Reflection Space
Partner A: One belief I bring into conflict is:	
Partner A: What I need you to understand is:	
Partner A: What I am working on is:	
Partner B: One belief I bring into conflict is:	
Partner B: What I need you to understand is:	
Partner B: What I am working on is:	
Shared reflection: What did we learn about each other's internal stories?	

CHAPTER REFLECTION

EXERCISE 3.8

Before You Begin
The purpose of this chapter is not to erase your history. The purpose is to stop letting unexamined stories control the present.

Prompt	Reflection Space
What did I learn about my mental models?	
Which belief seems to influence my conflict response the most?	
Which assumption do I make too quickly?	
What old story may still be active in the relationship?	
What inherited rule do I want to revise?	
What is one small action I can take this week to respond to the present moment rather than only to an old story?	

CHAPTER COMMITMENT

EXERCISE 3.9

Before You Begin
A learning relationship becomes stronger when both partners are willing to examine the stories they bring into love.

Prompt	Reflection Space
My small intentional action this week will be:	
I will know I practiced it when:	
One assumption I will test before reacting is:	
One old story I will notice with more care is:	
I will review this commitment on:	

CONCLUSION

Every relationship contains more than two people in the room. It contains histories, expectations, fears, inherited rules, cultural messages, previous injuries, and private definitions of what love should be. These forces do not always announce themselves. They appear through interpretation. They shape what each partner hears, what each partner fears, and what each partner believes the moment means. When these mental models remain hidden, conflict becomes harder to repair because the couple is not only disagreeing about the event; they are disagreeing through different realities.

The work of this chapter is to bring those realities into view. Once a mental model is named, it becomes less automatic. Once an assumption is tested, it becomes less controlling. Once a partner can say, "Here is the story that gets activated in me," the relationship gains a new kind of honesty. This honesty does not remove responsibility. It deepens it. Each partner becomes more accountable for the meanings they create, the reactions they repeat, and the old rules they continue to follow.

The next chapter moves from the stories partners carry into the personal work each partner must practice inside the relationship. Once mental models become visible, the question becomes more direct: What do I do with what I now understand about myself? Personal mastery is the discipline of becoming more aware, more responsible, and more intentional in the way you show up. A relationship cannot become a learning system if neither person is willing to keep learning themselves.

BECOMING A STRONGER PARTNER WITHOUT LOSING YOURSELF

PRACTICING PERSONAL MASTERY, EMOTIONAL AWARENESS, VALUES-BASED ACTION, AND SELF-RESPONSIBILITY INSIDE THE RELATIONSHIP.

CHAPTER FOCUS

This chapter helps you strengthen how you show up inside the relationship. You will examine triggers, automatic responses, boundaries, values, repair, and the small intentional actions that shape resilience.

CHAPTER 4

BECOMING A STRONGER PARTNER WITHOUT LOSING YOURSELF

Practicing personal mastery, emotional awareness, values-based action, and self-responsibility inside the relationship.

A relationship system cannot become healthier if the individuals inside it refuse to keep learning. Systems thinking helps a couple see the pattern, feedback loops help the couple understand how information moves through the relationship, and mental models reveal the stories each partner brings into conflict. Yet awareness alone is not enough. At some point, each person must ask a more personal question: "How am I showing up inside the system I say I want to improve?" This is the beginning of personal mastery.

Personal mastery does not mean perfection, emotional control at all times, or becoming the partner your spouse demands you to be. It means developing the capacity to observe yourself honestly, regulate your responses more intentionally, act from values rather than impulse, and take responsibility for your part in the relationship without surrendering your dignity. In Senge's learning organization framework, personal mastery involves the discipline of continual growth, self-awareness, and commitment to a meaningful vision (Senge, 2006). In a relationship, personal mastery becomes the practice of becoming a more conscious partner.

Many people enter relationship conflict focused almost entirely on what the other person needs to change. This is understandable, especially when there has been pain, disappointment, or repeated frustration. However, a relationship cannot grow if both partners wait for the other person to become different first. Personal mastery interrupts that waiting. It does not ask, "How can I force my partner to change?" It asks, "What is within my responsibility, my awareness, my behavior, my regulation, my repair, and my next intentional action?"

This distinction matters because personal mastery is often confused with self-blame. Self-blame says, "Everything is my fault." Personal mastery says, "I am responsible for what belongs to me." Self-blame collapses under shame. Personal mastery stands in accountability. Self-blame often leads to silence, resentment, or over-functioning. Personal mastery leads to clearer boundaries, better emotional regulation, and more intentional participation in the relationship system.

A learning relationship requires both partners to become more aware of their automatic responses. These responses may include criticism, withdrawal, defensiveness, people pleasing, emotional shutdown, overexplaining, rescuing, controlling, avoidance, sarcasm, or repeated apology without behavioral change. These behaviors are often protective. They may have helped a person survive earlier emotional environments, reduce conflict, preserve dignity, or avoid rejection. Yet a behavior that once protected the self may now weaken the relationship. Attachment theory reminds us that people often respond to closeness, threat, separation, and emotional uncertainty through patterns shaped by earlier relational experience (Bowlby, 1969; Hazan & Shaver, 1987).

Personal mastery begins with noticing the moment before the automatic response takes over. There is often a brief space between the trigger and the reaction. In that space, the body has already begun to respond. The chest tightens. The face changes. The stomach drops. The voice sharpens. The mind reaches for a familiar story. The partner becomes the problem. The conflict begins to feel inevitable. A stronger partner learns to notice this sequence earlier.

This is where present moment awareness becomes important. Acceptance and Commitment Therapy emphasize psychological flexibility, values, present moment awareness, and committed action, especially when difficult thoughts and feelings are present (Hayes et al., 2012). Applied to relationships, this means a person does not need to wait until they feel calm, confident, or perfectly understood before choosing a more constructive response. They can notice the discomfort and still act in alignment with the kind of partner they want to become.

The phrase "showing up" can sound simple, but in a relationship, it is one of the most demanding practices. Showing up means staying emotionally present without attacking. It means telling the truth without cruelty. It means listening when defensiveness is available. It means taking responsibility without collapsing into shame. It means pausing when the old pattern is inviting you back. Resilience is shaped in these small moments, not only in dramatic turning points.

Personal mastery also requires the ability to distinguish between feelings, urges, and values. A feeling may be anger. An urge may be to criticize. A value may be respect. A feeling may be fear. An urge may be to withdraw. A value may be connection. A feeling may be shame. An urge may be to defend. A value may be honesty. The work is not to deny the feeling. The work is to stop treating every urge as an instruction.

In long term relationships, partners often know each other's most sensitive places. This knowledge can become a form of care or a form of injury. A person with personal mastery does not use intimate knowledge as a weapon during conflict. They do not strike the place they know will hurt most simply because they feel wounded. They do not excuse harm by saying, "I was upset." Emotional intensity explains why a reaction may have happened, but it does not erase responsibility for the impact.

Personal mastery also includes the responsibility to know when you are not ready for a conversation. Some people continue speaking long after they have lost the capacity to listen. Others disappear emotionally without naming the need for space. A learning relationship benefits when each partner can say, "I want to continue this, but I need time to regulate first." The pause must not become abandonment, avoidance, or punishment. It should include a clear return point so the relationship knows the conversation is not being erased.

A stronger partner also learns to recognize the difference between a boundary and a defense. A boundary protects dignity, safety, values, and emotional health. A defense protects the ego from discomfort. A boundary may sound like, "I want to talk about this, but I will not continue if we are insulting each other." A defense may sound like, "I am not talking about this because you are too sensitive." Boundaries support a learning system because they create conditions where difficult conversations can happen without unnecessary damage.

Personal mastery is not only practiced during conflict. It is practiced in daily reliability. It appears in keeping agreements, following through, noticing emotional distance, offering appreciation, asking for clarification, repairing quickly, and choosing small behaviors that protect the relationship from unnecessary strain. Relationship maintenance research suggests that everyday practices such as positivity, openness, assurances, shared responsibilities, and connection with social networks are associated with healthier relationship functioning (Ogolsky & Bowers, 2013). Strong relationships are not sustained only by major declarations. They are sustained by repeated patterns of care.

There is also a resource dimension to personal mastery. Stress reduces capacity. Fatigue, financial pressure, grief, work demands, illness, and emotional overload can all weaken a person's ability to respond well. Conservation of Resources theory suggests that people strive to obtain, protect, and restore valued resources, and that stress becomes especially powerful when resources are threatened or lost (Hobfoll, 1989). In relationships, this means personal mastery must include resource awareness. A person who is depleted may need rest, support, planning, or repair before they can show up well.

This does not excuse harmful behavior under stress. It does mean that couples should pay attention to capacity. A partner who has slept poorly for weeks may become more reactive. A partner carrying invisible emotional labor may become less patient. A partner under financial strain may interpret ordinary questions as pressure. A learning relationship does not only ask, "Why did you react this way?" It also asks, "What conditions made this reaction more likely, and what can we change before it repeats?"

The exercises in this chapter will help you examine your own role in the relationship system. This work should be done with honesty and restraint. Do not use personal mastery as a reason to accept mistreatment. Do not use it as a reason to become the only person doing the work. Personal mastery is strongest when it exists alongside mutual accountability. You are responsible for your behavior, your growth, your repair, and your intentional action. You are not responsible for becoming the entire relationship by yourself.

EMOTIONAL TRIGGER MAP

EXERCISE 4.1

Before You Begin
This exercise helps you identify the moments when your automatic responses are most likely to appear. Complete this individually before discussing it with your partner.

Prompt	Reflection Space
I tend to feel triggered when my partner:	
I tend to feel triggered when the relationship feels:	
I tend to feel triggered when I believe:	
The emotion I usually feel first is:	
The emotion I show outwardly is:	
The reaction my partner usually sees is:	
The story that appears in my mind is:	
The behavior I usually choose is:	
The effect this has on the relationship is:	

My body usually signals distress through:	
My voice usually changes by:	
My thoughts usually become:	
My behavior usually shifts toward:	
A sign that I need to pause is:	
A sign that I am still able to continue the conversation is:	
When I notice my early warning signs, I can protect the relationship by:	

RESPONSIBILITY WITHOUT SELF BLAME

EXERCISE 4.2

Before You Begin

This exercise helps you identify what belongs to you without taking responsibility for what belongs to your partner.

Prompt	Reflection Space
A pattern I participate in is:	

My part in this pattern is:	
What I usually tell myself about my part is:	
What I need to acknowledge honestly is:	
What does not belong to me is:	
What does belong to me is:	
One behavior I need to change is:	
One repair I may need to offer is:	
One boundary I may need to hold is:	
Self-blame would say:	
Personal mastery would say:	
The responsible next step is:	

EXERCISE 4.3

Before You Begin

This exercise helps you connect your behavior during stress to the kind of partner you want to become.

Prompt	Reflection Space
When I am calm, I want to be a partner who is:	
When I am hurt, I usually become:	
When I am afraid, I usually become:	
When I am overwhelmed, I usually become:	
When I feel criticized, I usually become:	
The value I want to practice during conflict is:	
The behavior that would express this value is:	
The sentence I can use to return to this value is:	
The stressful moment is:	

My usual reaction would be:	
The value I want to practice is:	
A more intentional response would be:	
The small action I can take is:	

THE PAUSE AND RETURN PLAN

EXERCISE 4.4

Before You Begin
This exercise helps you create a pause that protects the relationship without abandoning the conversation.

Prompt	Reflection Space
I usually need a pause when:	
My signs of emotional flooding are:	
A harmful way I sometimes pause is:	
A healthier way I can ask for a pause is:	
The amount of time I usually need is:	

What I can do during the pause to regulate is:	
What I should avoid doing during the pause is:	
How I will return to the conversation is:	
When I feel overwhelmed, I will say:	
I am asking for this pause because:	
I will return to the conversation at:	
When I return, I will begin by saying:	

SMALL STEPS TOWARD RESILIENCE

EXERCISE 4.5

Before You Begin
This exercise helps translate personal mastery into small actions that can be practiced consistently.

Prompt	Reflection Space
One area where I want to show up more intentionally is:	

The smallest meaningful action I can take is:	
I can practice this action when:	
The obstacle I expect is:	
How I will respond to the obstacle is:	
How my partner may notice the change is:	
How I will know I am practicing resilience is:	
This week, I will practice:	
I will practice it at least:	
I will review the impact on:	

CHAPTER REFLECTION

EXERCISE 4.6

Before You Begin
Use this space before moving forward. The purpose is to integrate what you observed and identify the next small step.

Prompt	Reflection Space
What did I learn about my automatic responses?	
What trigger do I need to understand more carefully?	
What behavior do I need to take responsibility for?	
What value do I want to practice under stress?	
What is one boundary I may need to clarify?	
What is one way I can show up without losing myself?	
What small step would move me toward the kind of partner I want to become?	

EXERCISE 4.7

Before You Begin
A learning relationship requires partners who are willing to keep learning themselves. This week, I will practice personal mastery by noticing my reaction before I surrender to it.

Prompt	Reflection Space
My small intentional action this week will be:	
I will know I practiced it when:	
One value I will practice under pressure is:	
One repair I will make if needed is:	
I will review this commitment on:	

CONCLUSION

Personal mastery is not the work of becoming flawless. It is the work of becoming more awake inside the relationship. It asks each partner to notice the space between pain and reaction, between fear and defense, between old stories and present choices. This kind of awareness does not make conflict disappear. It gives the relationship a different kind of possibility when conflict arrives.

The strongest relationships are not built by people who never feel triggered, defensive, afraid, or overwhelmed. They are built by people who become increasingly able to recognize those states and choose with more intention. A partner who can pause before attacking, listen before defending, repair before resentment hardens, and act from values rather than impulse changes the emotional structure of the relationship. One small action may not transform the entire system, but repeated intentional actions begin to teach the system a new way to function.

The next chapter moves from individual responsibility to shared direction. Once each partner begins examining how they show up, the relationship must ask what it is trying to become. Without shared vision, two people can work hard and still move in different directions. Chapter 5 will guide you into the work of clarifying what you are building together.

DECIDING WHAT WE ARE BUILDING TOGETHER

CREATING SHARED VISION, ALIGNING VALUES, AND TURNING RELATIONSHIP GOALS INTO OBSERVABLE PRACTICES.

CHAPTER FOCUS

This chapter helps you identify what both partners are trying to build together so daily choices, decisions, and repair practices can align with a shared direction.

CHAPTER 5

DECIDING WHAT WE ARE BUILDING TOGETHER

Creating shared vision, aligning values, and turning relationship goals into observable practices.

A relationship can be active without being aligned. Two people can share a home, responsibilities, routines, memories, and obligations while quietly carrying different ideas about what the relationship is supposed to become. One partner may be working toward emotional closeness, while the other is working toward stability. One may define success as peace, while the other defines it as growth. One may want adventure, while the other wants predictability. Without shared vision, the relationship may remain busy but directionless.

Shared vision is one of the core disciplines in a learning organization because it creates a common direction that people can commit to rather than merely comply with (Senge, 2006). In business, a shared vision helps people understand what they are building, why it matters, and how individual decisions connect to the larger purpose. In a relationship, shared vision serves a similar function. It helps partners define the kind of life, connection, partnership, family culture, and emotional environment they are trying to create together.

Many couples assume they have a shared vision because they love each other or because they once agreed on major milestones. They may have agreed to marry, raise children, buy a home, support each other's careers, or remain faithful. These agreements matter, but they do not always create a living vision. A milestone is not the same as a direction. A couple may reach the milestone and still not know how they want to live, communicate, grow, repair, support, and make meaning together.

Shared vision requires more than shared logistics. It asks partners to define the quality of the relationship they want to build. Do we want a relationship that prioritizes emotional transparency? Do we want a relationship that values calm, privacy, faith, ambition, creativity, service, family, financial security, learning, adventure, or community? How do we want to treat each other when life becomes difficult? What kind of emotional climate do we want our home to carry? What do we want people to experience when they are close to us as a couple? What do we want to become together that neither of us could become alone?

This work matters because conflict often intensifies when partners are pursuing different visions without realizing it. A disagreement about spending may actually be a disagreement about security, freedom, status, sacrifice, or future planning. A disagreement about time may actually be a disagreement about connection, ambition, independence, or family identity. A disagreement about parenting may actually be a disagreement about values, discipline, protection, or the emotional culture of the home. The surface issue becomes easier to understand when the deeper vision is named.

Shared vision does not mean both partners become identical. A healthy relationship does not erase individuality. In fact, shared vision is strongest when both people can bring their honest desires into the conversation without being absorbed, dismissed, or dominated. The goal is not to create one partner's dream and force the other to support it. The goal is to build a relational direction that can hold both people's values with integrity.

Sternberg's triangular theory of love identifies intimacy, passion, and commitment as central components of love (Sternberg, 1986). Over time, couples may experience these dimensions differently, and each partner may prioritize them in different ways. One may long for deeper emotional intimacy. Another may be focused on commitment and reliability. Another may mourn the loss of passion or playfulness. Shared vision helps couples discuss these differences with maturity rather than assuming that love should automatically remain balanced without intentional care.

A relationship vision also protects couples from drifting into default settings. Without intentional vision, the relationship may be shaped mostly by stress, habit, family expectations, financial pressure, work demands, unresolved conflict, or cultural scripts. The couple may wake up years later and realize they have been reacting to life rather than building a life. Shared vision interrupts drift. It gives the relationship a reason to ask, "Does this decision move us toward who we say we want to become?"

This is not abstract work. Shared vision should eventually become practical. If a couple says they value connection, then connection must appear somewhere in their calendar, conversations, routines, and repair practices. If they say they value financial stability, then financial decisions must reflect shared responsibility and transparency. If they say they value growth, then each partner must make room for learning, feedback, and change. A vision that never becomes behavior is only language.

Relationship maintenance research supports the importance of ongoing behaviors that protect and strengthen connection, including openness, assurances, positivity, shared tasks, and attention to relational networks (Ogolsky & Bowers, 2013). These practices are not separate from vision. They are how vision becomes visible. A couple that values partnership must practice partnership in the ordinary details of life. A couple that values respect must practice respect when disappointed. A couple that values resilience must practice repair when the system is strained.

Shared vision also helps couples make decisions during stress. When pressure increases, people often retreat into self-protection. One partner may focus on survival, while the other focuses on control. One may become urgent, while the other becomes avoidant. A clear shared vision gives the couple a reference point when emotions become loud. It allows them to ask, "What kind of couple do we want to be in this moment?" This question does not solve every problem, but it can interrupt reactions that violate the relationship's deeper values.

A strong shared vision must include both aspiration and honesty. Couples should not write a vision that sounds beautiful but ignores the real condition of the relationship. If trust has been damaged, the vision should include rebuilding trust. If communication has become defensive, the vision should include learning safer feedback. If intimacy has weakened, the vision should include understanding what intimacy now requires. A mature vision does not pretend the relationship is already what it hopes to become. It names the direction and the work.

The exercises in this chapter will help you clarify individual values, compare visions, identify areas of alignment and misalignment, and create a relationship mission statement. This process may reveal differences that feel uncomfortable. That is not failure. Differences become dangerous when they remain hidden. A learning relationship does not require perfect sameness. It requires enough honesty to understand where each partner is standing and enough commitment to decide how to move forward together.

INDIVIDUAL RELATIONSHIP VISION

EXERCISE 5.1

Before You Begin
Complete this exercise individually before discussing your answers with your partner.

Prompt	Reflection Space
The kind of relationship I want to build is:	
When I imagine us at our healthiest, I see:	
I want our relationship to feel like:	
I want our home or shared life to feel like:	
I want us to handle conflict by:	
I want us to handle stress by:	
I want us to support individual growth by:	
I want us to protect connection by:	

I want us to make decisions by:	
I want us to repair harm by:	
The three values I most want our relationship to reflect are:	
Value one:	
Value two:	
Value three:	
One thing I need more of in our shared future is:	
One thing I need less of in our shared future is:	
One thing I am willing to contribute to this vision is:	

SHARED VALUES ALIGNMENT

EXERCISE 5.2

Before You Begin
Use this exercise together after each partner completes Exercise 5.1.

Prompt	Reflection Space
Partner A top three values:	
Partner B top three values:	
Values we clearly share:	
Values that are different but compatible:	
Values that may create tension:	
A value we talk about but do not practice consistently is:	
A value we practice well is:	
A value that needs clearer behavior is:	
Shared value:	
What this value looks like during ordinary life:	
What this value looks like during conflict:	

What this value looks like during stress:	
What this value looks like during repair:	
One behavior that would violate this value is:	
One behavior that would strengthen this value is:	

RELATIONSHIP MISSION STATEMENT

EXERCISE 5.3

Before You Begin
A mission statement gives the relationship a clear direction. Keep it honest, specific, and realistic.

Prompt	Reflection Space
Our relationship exists to create:	
We want to become a couple who:	
We want our love to be known for:	
We will protect:	
We will practice:	

We will repair:	
We will keep learning by:	
Our relationship mission is:	
Does this statement reflect both partners?	
Is it specific enough to guide behavior?	
Is it honest about the work ahead?	
What word or phrase needs to be revised?	
Final relationship mission statement:	

FUTURE US REFLECTION

EXERCISE 5.4

Before You Begin
This exercise helps you imagine the relationship as a long-term system.

Prompt	Reflection Space
Imagine the relationship five years from now if it continues repeating its current patterns. What would likely be stronger?	

What would likely be weaker?	
What issue might become more serious?	
What emotional distance might grow?	
What would we regret not addressing sooner?	
Imagine the relationship five years from now if both partners practice learning, repair, and shared vision. What would likely be stronger?	
What would feel different between us?	
What practices would we have built?	
What would we be proud of?	
What would our future selves thank us for starting now?	
The future we want requires us to begin practicing:	

DECISION ALIGNMENT CHECKLIST

EXERCISE 5.5

Before You Begin
Use this checklist when making important decisions.

Prompt	Reflection Space
The decision we are considering is:	
Which shared value does this decision support?	
Which shared value might this decision strain?	
How does this decision affect each partner?	
How does this decision affect the relationship system?	
How does this decision affect our long-term vision?	
What fear may be influencing this decision?	
What hope may be influencing this decision?	
What information do we still need?	

What agreement would help us move forward with respect?	
Final decision or next step:	

CHAPTER REFLECTION

EXERCISE 5.6

Before You Begin

Use this space before moving forward. The purpose is to integrate what you observed and identify the next small step.

Prompt	Reflection Space
What did I learn about my vision for the relationship?	
Where are we most aligned?	
Where are we misaligned?	
What value needs more action?	
What part of our shared future feels hopeful?	
What part of our shared future needs careful attention?	
What is one decision we need to revisit through the lens of shared vision?	

EXERCISE 5.7

Before You Begin
A learning relationship needs direction. This week, I will practice making one small choice that reflects the relationship we say we want to build.

Prompt	Reflection Space
My small intentional action this week will be:	
I will know I practiced it when:	
One shared value I will honor is:	
One behavior that will make this value visible is:	
I will review this commitment on:	

CONCLUSION

Shared vision gives love direction. It allows a couple to move beyond survival, habit, and reaction into intentional design. Without vision, a relationship may still function, but it may function according to stress, convenience, avoidance, or inherited rules. With vision, the couple gains a way to ask whether their daily choices are building the relationship they claim to want.

The purpose of this chapter was not to create a perfect statement that sounds impressive on paper. The purpose was to clarify what matters and what must become visible through action. A relationship vision only has power when it becomes behavior. The relationship becomes stronger when both partners can say, "This is what we are building, and this is how I will help build it."

The next chapter moves from shared direction into shared pressure. It is one thing to define a vision when life is calm. It is another thing to practice that vision when stress arrives. Chapter 6 will focus on team learning during stress, especially the shift from coping alone to coping as a coordinated relational system.

LEARNING TOGETHER UNDER PRESSURE

USING TEAM LEARNING AND DYADIC COPING TO RESPOND TO STRESS AS A COORDINATED RELATIONSHIP SYSTEM.

CHAPTER FOCUS

This chapter is for shifting from solo coping to shared coping during stress. This chapter helps you understand stress responses, support preferences, dyadic coping, and the practices that allow the relationship to function as a team under pressure.

CHAPTER 6

LEARNING TOGETHER UNDER PRESSURE

Using team learning and dyadic coping to respond to stress as a coordinated relationship system.

Stress reveals the operating system of a relationship. When life is calm, many couples can appear connected, generous, patient, and aligned. Pressure tests whether those qualities are practiced deeply enough to remain available when resources are strained. Financial uncertainty, illness, grief, parenting demands, work overload, family conflict, relocation, disappointment, and unexpected change all place weight on the relationship system. The question is not whether stress will come. The question is whether the relationship knows how to learn while stress is present.

Team learning is one of the disciplines of a learning organization because groups must learn how to think, communicate, coordinate, and adjust together (Senge, 2006). In a relationship, team learning means the couple develops the capacity to face pressure as a coordinated unit rather than two isolated individuals fighting for emotional survival. This does not mean partners lose individuality or that every stressor must be handled in exactly the same way. It means they learn how to understand each other's stress responses, share information, offer support, and adjust together.

Many couples struggle under pressure because stress narrows attention. A person under stress may become more focused on immediate survival than relational connection. One partner may become task oriented, while the other needs emotional reassurance. One may want to talk, while the other needs quiet. One may seek closeness, while the other seeks control. These differences can become secondary stressors. The original problem remains, but now the couple is also distressed by how differently they are responding to the problem.

Dyadic coping research is especially useful here because it examines how couples respond to stress together. Bodenmann's systemic transactional model emphasizes that stress in one partner can affect both partners and that couples may respond through supportive, delegated, common, or negative coping patterns (Bodenmann, 2005). A relationship becomes stronger when partners can recognize stress as something influencing the system, not merely something belonging to one individual.

The movement from solo coping to shared coping is central to long term resilience. Solo coping says, "I have to handle this by myself." Shared coping says, "This pressure is affecting us, and we need to understand how to face it together." This does not mean every problem becomes equally shared. Some responsibilities may still belong primarily to one partner. However, the emotional meaning of the stress becomes visible to the relationship. The partner under pressure is not left alone inside the system.

Couples often misread each other's stress responses. A partner who becomes quiet may be trying to regulate, but the other may experience the silence as rejection. A partner who asks many questions may be trying to create a plan, but the other may experience the questions as criticism. A partner who becomes emotional may be seeking connection, but the other may experience the emotion as escalation. A partner who becomes practical may be trying to help, but the other may experience practicality as emotional dismissal. Without team learning, stress responses become personal accusations.

Research on dyadic coping suggests that how couples cope together is associated with relationship satisfaction and well-being over time (Rusu et al., 2020). Systematic review work also shows that dyadic coping is meaningfully connected to individual and relational outcomes, especially when couples face mental health concerns or significant stressors (Landolt et al., 2023). These findings support one of the central claims of this workbook: relationships do not become resilient because stress is absent. They become resilient when the couple develops ways to respond to stress with shared awareness and adaptive support.

A learning relationship must also recognize that support is not one size fits all. One partner may feel supported by practical help. Another may feel supported by verbal reassurance. One may need problem solving. Another may need presence before solutions. One may need space. Another may need touch. One may need help organizing tasks. Another may need the partner to acknowledge the emotional weight of the situation. Support becomes more effective when partners learn what kind of support actually helps rather than offering only the kind of support they personally prefer.

This distinction can prevent many avoidable conflicts. A practical partner may believe they are being helpful by offering solutions, while the other partner feels emotionally unseen. An emotionally expressive partner may believe they are creating closeness by talking through the problem, while the other partner feels overwhelmed. Neither partner may intend harm. The problem is that support is being offered without enough knowledge of the receiver's needs. Team learning asks couples to study support as carefully as they study conflict.

Stress also affects feedback loops and mental models. Under pressure, feedback may sound harsher, defensiveness may rise faster, old stories may activate more easily, and shared vision may temporarily disappear. A couple that understands this can prepare for stress instead of being surprised by it every time. They can ask, "What happens to us when we are under pressure?" This question is more useful than waiting until the system is already overloaded.

Conservation of Resources theory suggests that stress is deeply connected to the threat or loss of valued resources such as energy, time, emotional stability, finances, health, and social support (Hobfoll, 1989). In relationships, these resources are not only individual. They become relational. A couple may lose time together, emotional patience, financial security, trust, intimacy, or the felt sense of being on the same team. Resilience requires noticing resource loss early and making intentional choices to protect what remains.

Team learning during stress does not mean every stressful moment becomes a long conversation. Sometimes the relationship needs action first. Sometimes bills must be paid, children must be cared for, a doctor must be called, a decision must be made, or a deadline must be met. But even in action, the couple can communicate as a team. They can clarify roles, name emotional capacity, check assumptions, and return later to process what happened. The relationship does not need to stop functioning in order to feel. It needs a way to do both.

A relationship review after stress can be especially powerful. Many couples move past stressful events without learning from them. They survive the crisis, feel relief, and then return to ordinary life without asking what the stress revealed. As a result, the same weaknesses reappear in the next crisis. A learning relationship asks different questions after pressure passes. What did we do well? Where did we feel alone? What support helped? What support missed? What pattern returned? What do we need to adjust before the next stressful season?

The exercises in this chapter will help you identify stress responses, support preferences, shared coping patterns, and post stress learning practices. This work should be approached with patience. Stress can expose vulnerable areas in the relationship, and some couples may discover that they have been coping beside each other rather than with each other. That discovery may be painful, but it is also useful. Once the pattern is visible, the couple can begin designing a better response.

STRESS RESPONSE COMPARISON

EXERCISE 6.1

Before You Begin
Complete this exercise individually first, then compare your answers with your partner.

Prompt	Reflection Space
When I am under stress, I usually become:	
When I am under stress, I need:	
When I am under stress, I tend to avoid:	
When I am under stress, I usually communicate by:	
When I am under stress, I may unintentionally make my partner feel:	
When my partner is under stress, I usually assume:	
When my partner is under stress, I tend to respond by:	
What I often misunderstand about my partner's stress response is:	
What I want my partner to understand about my stress response is:	

Where are our stress responses similar?	
Where are our stress responses different?	
How might our differences create conflict?	
How might our differences help the relationship?	
One stress response we need to understand better is:	

SOLO COPING VERSUS SHARED COPING

EXERCISE 6.2

Before You Begin
This exercise helps identify whether stress is being handled individually, jointly, or in conflict.

Prompt	Reflection Space
The stressor was:	
How I coped individually:	
How my partner coped individually:	

How we coped together:	
Where I felt supported:	
Where I felt alone:	
Where my partner may have felt supported:	
Where my partner may have felt alone:	
What we did well as a team:	
What we did not discuss clearly:	
What the stress revealed about our relationship system:	
During stress, I tend to move toward solo coping when:	
During stress, we move toward shared coping when:	
One way we can shift from solo coping to shared coping is:	

SUPPORT PREFERENCE INVENTORY

EXERCISE 6.3

Before You Begin

This exercise helps each partner identify what kind of support is most useful.

Prompt	Reflection Space
When I am stressed, practical help feels:	
When I am stressed, emotional reassurance feels:	
When I am stressed, physical affection feels:	
When I am stressed, advice feels:	
When I am stressed, quiet presence feels:	
When I am stressed, questions feel:	
When I am stressed, space feels:	
When I am stressed, problem solving feels:	
The support I most often need first is:	

The support I usually need later is:	
The support that often does not help me is:	
The support I forget to ask for is:	
A clear way I can ask for support is:	
When Partner A is stressed, helpful support includes:	
When Partner B is stressed, helpful support includes:	
A support behavior we will practice this week is:	

PRESSURE COMMUNICATION SCRIPT

EXERCISE 6.4

Before You Begin
Use this script during a stressful moment or shortly after one.

Prompt	Reflection Space
The stressor we are facing is:	

What feels most urgent is:	
What feels emotionally difficult is:	
What I need you to understand is:	
What I need from you right now is:	
What I can offer right now is:	
What I do not have capacity for right now is:	
The decision we need to make is:	
The support we need outside the relationship is:	
The next right step is:	
Even though this is stressful, we can protect the relationship by:	

AFTER THE STORM REVIEW

EXERCISE 6.5

Before You Begin
Use this exercise after a stressful event has passed or decreased.

Prompt	Reflection Space
The stressful event was:	
What did we handle well?	
Where did we become disconnected?	
Where did one or both partners feel alone?	
What support helped?	
What support missed the mark?	
What assumptions did we make?	

What feedback loop broke down?	
What mental model was activated?	
What personal mastery skill was needed?	
What shared value did we practice?	
What shared value did we forget?	
What should we do differently next time?	
One lesson our relationship can learn from this stressor is:	

CHAPTER REFLECTION

EXERCISE 6.6

Before You Begin
Use this space before moving forward. The purpose is to integrate what you observed and identify the next small step.

Prompt	Reflection Space
What did I learn about my stress response?	
What did I learn about my partner's stress response?	
Where do we cope well together?	
Where do we become isolated under stress?	
What kind of support do I need to ask for more clearly?	
What kind of support does my partner need that I may overlook?	
What pattern do we need to interrupt during pressure?	
What is one small action we can take to become a better team under stress?	

EXERCISE 6.7

Before You Begin
A learning relationship does not wait for stress to disappear before practicing resilience. This week, I will practice becoming more aware of how I respond under pressure and how I can support the relationship system.

Prompt	Reflection Space
My small intentional action this week will be:	
I will know I practiced it when:	
One stress signal I will notice is:	
One support behavior I will practice is:	
One way I will move from solo coping to shared coping is:	
I will review this commitment on:	

CONCLUSION

Stress does not create every relationship problem, but it often reveals the patterns that were already present. It shows how partners communicate when capacity is low, how they interpret each other when fear is high, and how quickly the system moves toward isolation or teamwork. This is why stress must be treated as part of the relationship system rather than only as an outside burden. A couple that learns under pressure becomes more prepared for the next season of difficulty.

The goal is not to eliminate stress from love. That would be impossible. The goal is to build a relationship that can remain connected enough to learn while stress is present. When partners understand each other's stress responses, ask for support clearly, offer help in ways the other can receive, and review difficult seasons after they pass, the relationship becomes more resilient. It becomes less dependent on ideal conditions and more capable of intentional action in real life.

The next chapter turns this learning into a repeated practice. A relationship cannot rely only on crisis conversations or emotional breakthroughs. It needs a rhythm for review, reflection, repair, and realignment. Chapter 7 introduces the relationship review meeting, a structured practice for helping the relationship continue learning before small issues become major breakdowns.

THE RELATIONSHIP REVIEW MEETING

CREATING A REPEATABLE RHYTHM OF REVIEW, REPAIR, APPRECIATION, AND REALIGNMENT.

CHAPTER FOCUS

This chapter is emphasis on creating a repeatable rhythm of reflection, repair, and realignment. This chapter helps you create structured relationship review meetings that allow the relationship to notice patterns, offer feedback, make repairs, and choose the next right step.

CHAPTER 7

THE RELATIONSHIP REVIEW MEETING

Creating a repeatable rhythm of review, repair, appreciation, and realignment.

A relationship that wants to keep learning needs a rhythm for review. Many couples wait until conflict becomes painful before they talk about the condition of the relationship. They discuss communication only after communication has broken down. They discuss emotional distance only after distance has become difficult to ignore. They discuss stress only after stress has already shaped the tone of the home. This reactive pattern places too much pressure on crisis conversations. A learning relationship needs a more intentional structure.

In business, review meetings are used to examine performance, identify problems, clarify priorities, strengthen accountability, and adjust strategy before small issues become larger failures. The purpose is not to create blame. The purpose is to make the system visible. A team cannot improve what it refuses to examine. A relationship works in a similar way. Without a regular practice of reflection, partners may assume the relationship is fine simply because no one has named a problem. Silence may be mistaken for peace. Routine may be mistaken for connection. Avoidance may be mistaken for stability.

A relationship review meeting is a structured conversation designed to help partners pause, listen, assess, repair, and realign. It is not a courtroom, a complaint session, a performance evaluation, or an opportunity to reopen every unresolved wound at once. It is a learning practice. The meeting gives the relationship a predictable space to ask what is working, what needs attention, what each partner is carrying, what support is needed, and what small adjustment should happen next.

This practice draws from several parts of the learning relationship framework. Systems thinking helps the couple examine patterns rather than isolated incidents. Feedback loops help the couple understand what signals have appeared. Mental models help partners notice the assumptions shaping their interpretations. Personal mastery helps each person take responsibility for how they show up. Shared vision reminds the couple what they are building. Team learning helps them coordinate under stress. The relationship review meeting brings these disciplines into a repeated rhythm (Senge, 2006).

The meeting must be emotionally safe enough to become sustainable. Psychological safety was originally studied in work teams, where learning depends on whether people feel able to raise concerns, admit mistakes, and take interpersonal risks without fear of humiliation or punishment (Edmondson, 1999). In a relationship, the principle is similar. If one partner fears that honesty will be punished, mocked, dismissed, or used later as ammunition, the review meeting will not produce learning. It will produce guarded performance. The goal is not to force vulnerability. The goal is to create a structure where honesty has a better chance of being received.

Couples often resist structured relationship meetings because the idea can feel formal or unnatural. They may believe love should not require scheduled review. Yet many of the most important parts of adult life are protected by structure. People schedule medical visits, financial reviews, work meetings, spiritual practices, family routines, and personal responsibilities because what matters requires attention. A relationship is not weakened by structure. It is often weakened by assuming that connection will maintain itself without structure.

The meeting should be predictable but not rigid. Some couples may benefit from a weekly check in. Others may prefer a monthly review with shorter informal check ins between meetings. Couples under significant stress may need more frequent review. Couples in a stable season may need less. The point is not to follow one universal schedule. The point is to create a dependable rhythm where the relationship is observed before resentment, confusion, or distance becomes too large.

Relationship review meetings should include appreciation. This is not sentimental decoration. Appreciation helps the system notice what is working. Relationship maintenance research suggests that positive relational behaviors, assurances, openness, shared responsibilities, and everyday practices of connection are associated with stronger relationship functioning (Ogolsky & Bowers, 2013). If a couple only reviews problems, the meeting becomes emotionally exhausting. A learning relationship must study strengths as well as strain. What is repeated can be reinforced. What is appreciated can become more visible.

The meeting should also include stress review. Stress often changes the emotional climate of the relationship before partners realize what has happened. One partner may become sharper. The other may become quieter. Affection may decrease. Patience may narrow. Small issues may begin carrying more emotional weight. Conservation of Resources theory suggests that stress is connected to the threat or loss of valued resources such as time, energy, security, emotional steadiness, and support (Hobfoll, 1989). A review meeting gives couples a place to ask which resources are being strained and what support is needed before depletion becomes conflict.

The review meeting should not try to solve every issue immediately. This is one of the most common mistakes. A couple sits down to talk and opens too many emotional files at once. The conversation becomes overloaded, and both people leave feeling discouraged. A useful meeting identifies priorities. Some concerns need immediate action. Some need more discussion later. Some simply need to be named. Some require professional support. A learning relationship does not confuse urgency with importance. It learns to decide what must be addressed now and what should be scheduled for deeper attention.

The review meeting should include repair. Repair does not always require a dramatic apology. Sometimes repair begins with acknowledgment. A partner may say, I see that I dismissed your concern, or I understand that my silence felt like distance. Repair becomes stronger when it includes changed behavior. An apology without adjustment may temporarily reduce tension, but it does not teach the system anything new.

Structured relationship programs and relationship education have been associated with improvements in couple satisfaction and communication, although outcomes depend on the program, the couple's circumstances, and the quality of implementation (Javadivala et al., 2021). This matters because the review meeting is not a magic solution. It is a practice. Its value comes from repetition, emotional honesty, and follow through. A couple that meets but does not listen will not learn. A couple that listens but does not adjust will remain stuck.

The review meeting should end with one next right step. Not five. Not ten. One clear action that moves the relationship in the direction of health. This protects the couple from becoming overwhelmed. It also honors the reality that resilience is shaped through intentional action in the present moment. The relationship does not need to solve every difficulty in one conversation. It needs to practice one step that teaches the system something different.

The exercises in this chapter will help you design a relationship review meeting that fits your relationship. You will create a weekly check in, a monthly review, a repair practice, and a next step agreement. The goal is not to make your relationship feel like a business meeting. The goal is to create a protected space where love can think, speak, listen, and adjust.

WEEKLY CHECK IN

EXERCISE 7.1

Before You Begin
Use this exercise once a week. Keep the conversation brief enough to repeat consistently.

Prompt	Reflection Space
What felt strong between us this week?	
Where did we feel connected?	
Where did we feel distant?	
What stress affected the relationship this week?	
What feedback signal appeared this week?	
What did we handle well?	
What needs attention before it grows?	
What is one appreciation I want to offer?	
What is one small repair I need to make?	
What is one action we will practice before the next check in?	

MONTHLY RELATIONSHIP REVIEW

EXERCISE 7.2

Before You Begin
Use this exercise once a month to examine the broader relationship system.

Prompt	Reflection Space
This month, our relationship system felt:	
The strongest part of the relationship this month was:	
The most strained part of the relationship this month was:	
A recurring pattern we noticed was:	
A feedback loop that worked well was:	
A feedback loop that broke down was:	
A stressor that affected us was:	
A shared value we practiced was:	
A shared value we neglected was:	
One agreement we need to update is:	

APPRECIATION AND REPAIR PRACTICE

EXERCISE 7.3

Before You Begin
Use this exercise to balance recognition of strengths with responsibility for harm.

Prompt	Reflection Space
Partner A: One thing I appreciated about you recently was:	
Partner A: The impact it had on me was:	
Partner B: One thing I appreciated about you recently was:	
Partner B: The impact it had on me was:	
Partner A: One thing I need to acknowledge is:	
Partner A: What I want to do differently is:	
Partner B: One thing I need to acknowledge is:	
Partner B: What I want to do differently is:	
Shared reflection: What did appreciation make easier to discuss?	
What repair still needs follow through?	

WHAT IS WORKING AND WHAT NEEDS ATTENTION

EXERCISE 7.4

Before You Begin
This exercise helps the relationship examine strengths and concerns without becoming problem saturated.

Prompt	Reflection Space
What is currently working in our communication?	
What needs attention in our communication?	
What is currently working in our emotional connection?	
What needs attention in our emotional connection?	
What is currently working in our shared responsibilities?	
What needs attention in our shared responsibilities?	
What is currently working in how we handle stress?	
What needs attention in how we handle stress?	
The area that needs the most immediate attention is:	
The area that deserves appreciation is:	

NEXT RIGHT STEP AGREEMENT

EXERCISE 7.5

Before You Begin
Use this exercise at the end of each review meeting.

Prompt	Reflection Space
The issue we are addressing is:	
The pattern we noticed is:	
The small action we agree to practice is:	
Who will do what?	
When will this happen?	
What support is needed?	
How will we know it was practiced?	
When will we review it?	
What should we do if we do not follow through?	
Our next right step is:	

CHAPTER REFLECTION

EXERCISE 7.6

Before You Begin
Use this space before moving forward. The goal is to identify one realistic review habit the relationship can maintain.

Prompt	Reflection Space
What did I learn about how we review the relationship?	
What makes relationship review difficult for me?	
What makes relationship review useful for me?	
What kind of structure would help us talk more safely?	
What do I need to practice during review conversations?	
What does my partner need from me during review conversations?	
What is one review habit we can realistically maintain?	

CHAPTER COMMITMENT

EXERCISE 7.7

Before You Begin
A learning relationship needs a rhythm of review. This week, practice entering relationship conversations with curiosity, specificity, and responsibility.

Prompt	Reflection Space
My small intentional action this week will be:	
I will know I practiced it when:	
One appreciation I will offer is:	
One repair I will make if needed is:	
One next right step I will support is:	
I will review this commitment on:	

CONCLUSION

A relationship review meeting gives the relationship a place to listen before crisis demands attention. It helps partners notice patterns, name stress, offer appreciation, make repairs, and choose intentional action. The meeting is not valuable because it is formal. It is valuable because it protects learning from being left to chance.

The strongest couples are not those who never need review. They are often the couples willing to return to the relationship with honesty, humility, and discipline. They understand that love can drift when it is not examined. They understand that small issues become larger when they are repeatedly avoided. They understand that repair becomes more possible when the relationship has a rhythm for returning to itself.

The next chapter brings the workbook's main framework together. After learning to see the system, repair feedback loops, examine mental models, practice personal mastery, create shared vision, learn under stress, and hold review meetings, the relationship is ready to create a long-term resilience plan. Chapter 8 will guide you in designing a relationship system that can continue learning beyond this workbook.

THE RESILIENT RELATIONSHIP SYSTEM

BUILDING LONG TERM RESILIENCE THROUGH AWARENESS, REPAIR, PROTECTION, AND INTENTIONAL ACTION.

CHAPTER FOCUS

This chapter is for building long-term resilience through intentional action and continued learning. This chapter helps you bring the full learning relationship framework together into a practical long-term resilience plan.

CHAPTER 8

THE RESILIENT RELATIONSHIP SYSTEM

Building long term resilience through awareness, repair, protection, and intentional action.

Resilience is often misunderstood as the ability to endure without being affected. In relationships, this misunderstanding can be costly. A resilient relationship is not one where partners never struggle, never hurt each other, never disagree, or never face seasons of distance. It is not a relationship that appears calm because no one is telling the truth. It is not a relationship that survives by avoiding every difficult conversation. A resilient relationship is one that can experience strain, notice what is happening, respond with intention, repair with responsibility, and continue learning.

This workbook has treated the relationship as a living system. A living system must adapt. It must receive information, examine patterns, clarify assumptions, protect resources, and adjust behavior. When a relationship cannot adapt, it becomes fragile. It may appear stable for a time, but pressure exposes the weak points. A couple may keep repeating familiar conflict, avoiding necessary conversations, misunderstanding each other's needs, or losing connection under stress. The relationship may continue, but it may not be learning.

Resilience begins with awareness. A couple cannot strengthen a pattern they cannot see. Systems thinking helped you examine the relationship as more than isolated events. Feedback loops helped you notice how the relationship receives or rejects important signals. Mental models helped you identify the stories and assumptions that shape conflict. Personal mastery helped you examine your own responsibility inside the system. Shared vision helped you clarify what you are building. Team learning helped you understand how stress affects the relationship. Review meetings helped you create a rhythm for continued reflection. These disciplines now come together in the resilient relationship system (Senge, 2006).

Conservation of Resources theory suggests that stress becomes especially powerful when valued resources are threatened or lost, and that people work to protect, restore, and build resources over time (Hobfoll, 1989). In a relationship, resources include trust, time, emotional safety, affection, shared meaning, patience, financial stability, health, social support, and confidence in repair. A resilient relationship does not wait until these resources are depleted before paying attention. It learns to identify warning signs early.

Warning signs are not evidence of failure. They are information. A decrease in affection may be a warning sign. So may repeated irritability, emotional numbness, avoidance of certain topics, loss of playfulness, poor sleep, increased criticism, financial secrecy, withdrawal from shared routines, or the quiet belief that talking will not help. When couples treat warning signs as information rather than embarrassment, they can intervene earlier. The relationship becomes less dependent on emergency repair and more capable of preventive care.

Dyadic coping research shows that the way couples respond to stress together is associated with relationship satisfaction and relational functioning over time (Bodenmann, 2005; Rusu et al., 2020). This matters because resilience is not only an individual process. One partner's stress can enter the relationship system and affect both people. The couple's ability to recognize stress, communicate support needs, and respond together becomes part of the relationship's resilience. Stress does not have to divide the relationship, but it often will if the couple has no shared process for facing it.

Long term resilience also depends on repair. Repair is the process by which partners return to the relationship after injury, misunderstanding, distance, or conflict. Repair may include apology, explanation, changed behavior, reassurance, accountability, restitution, or renewed agreement. Repair is not complete simply because one person says they are sorry. Repair becomes meaningful when the relationship learns something from the harm and adjusts accordingly.

Some couples confuse forgiveness with repair. Forgiveness may be part of the healing process, but forgiveness alone does not redesign the system. A person may forgive and still need new boundaries. A person may forgive and still need time to rebuild trust. A person may forgive and still need the partner to change a repeated behavior. A resilient relationship does not pressure people to move past pain before the system has learned from it. It treats repair as both emotional and behavioral.

A strong resilience plan must include rituals of connection. Rituals do not need to be elaborate. They may include a morning greeting, a weekly walk, a shared meal without phones, a Sunday planning conversation, a gratitude practice, a bedtime check-in, a monthly review, or a consistent way of reconnecting after stress. Rituals give the relationship repeated evidence that connection matters. They also create stability during seasons when emotions are less predictable.

Positive emotion research suggests that positive emotional experiences can broaden perspective and help build enduring psychological and social resources over time (Fredrickson, 2001). In relationships, this does not mean forced positivity or denial of pain. It means that joy, appreciation, humor, warmth, and affection are not optional luxuries. They are relational resources. Couples who only discuss problems may become skilled at analysis but starved for connection. Resilience requires both truth and nourishment.

The resilient relationship system also protects individuality. Some couples mistake unity for sameness. They believe resilience means always agreeing, always coping the same way, or always needing the same things. But long-term love requires room for two developing people. Shared vision does not erase personal growth. Team learning does not eliminate individual responsibility. Personal mastery does not demand self-abandonment. A resilient relationship allows both partners to continue becoming while remaining meaningfully connected.

A resilience plan should include early intervention. Couples often know what happens before things deteriorate, but they do not formalize that knowledge. They know that conflict increases when sleep decreases. They know that intimacy suffers when schedules become overloaded. They know that money conversations become harder when information is delayed. They know that extended family stress affects the tone between them. A resilient system names these patterns and creates early responses. It does not wait for predictable breakdowns to become emergencies.

The relationship must also know when outside support is needed. A workbook can help couples reflect, communicate, and practice new patterns, but it cannot replace professional support when problems involve abuse, coercive control, active addiction, repeated betrayal, trauma, severe mental health concerns, intimidation, or ongoing emotional harm. Seeking support is not a failure of resilience. It can be an expression of resilience. Sometimes the most responsible action is to bring trained help into the system.

Your dissertation work on marital resilience and spousal support during shared stressors gives this workbook an important scholarly foundation. Long term relationship resilience is not built only through affection. It is shaped through how partners perceive support, experience stress together, regulate emotion, and make meaning during difficult seasons (Smith, 2026). This aligns with the central philosophy of this workbook: resilience is the choice to show up through intentional actions in the present moment. It is shaped through small steps in the right direction, repeated over time.

The exercises in this chapter will help you create a relationship resilience plan. You will identify warning signs, protective practices, repair rituals, growth commitments, and support needs. This final chapter is not the end of the work. It is the beginning of a repeatable system. The goal is for the relationship to continue learning after the workbook closes.

RELATIONSHIP RESILIENCE PLAN

EXERCISE 8.1

Before You Begin
Use this exercise to create an overview of your relationship resilience system.

Prompt	Reflection Space
Our relationship is strongest when:	
Our relationship is most vulnerable when:	
The patterns that place us at risk are:	
The strengths that protect us are:	
The stressors we need to monitor are:	
The resources we need to protect are:	
The support practices that help us are:	
The repair practices we need to strengthen are:	
The shared values that should guide us are:	
Our relationship resilience statement is:	

WARNING SIGNS AND EARLY INTERVENTIONS

EXERCISE 8.2

Before You Begin
Identify signs that the relationship system needs attention, then decide what action should happen earlier next time.

Prompt	Reflection Space
Early warning signs in our relationship include:	
A warning sign I tend to minimize is:	
A warning sign my partner may notice before I do is:	
A warning sign that usually appears before conflict is:	
A warning sign that usually appears before distance is:	
When we notice emotional distance, we will:	
When we notice repeated irritability, we will:	
When we notice avoidance, we will:	
When we notice unresolved conflict, we will:	
When we notice one partner becoming overwhelmed, we will:	

REPAIR RITUAL DESIGN

EXERCISE 8.3

Before You Begin
A repair ritual helps the relationship return after conflict, distance, or injury.

Prompt	Reflection Space
After conflict, I usually need:	
After conflict, my partner usually needs:	
A repair attempt that helps me is:	
A repair attempt that does not help me is:	
A phrase we can use to begin repair is:	
A behavior that should accompany apology is:	
A way we can check whether repair is complete is:	
Our repair ritual will include step one:	
Our repair ritual will include step two:	
We will use this ritual when:	

PROTECTIVE PRACTICES

EXERCISE 8.4

Before You Begin
Protective practices help prevent unnecessary relational erosion.

Prompt	Reflection Space
A daily practice that would strengthen connection is:	
A weekly practice that would strengthen connection is:	
A monthly practice that would strengthen alignment is:	
A stress practice that would protect the relationship is:	
A communication practice we need to maintain is:	
A support practice we need to maintain is:	
An appreciation practice we need to maintain is:	
A boundary that protects the relationship is:	
A habit that weakens the relationship and should be reduced is:	
The protective practice we will begin first is:	

GROWTH COMMITMENTS FOR EACH PARTNER

EXERCISE 8.5

Before You Begin
Each partner identifies personal growth commitments that support the relationship system.

Prompt	Reflection Space
Partner A: The pattern I am working to change is:	
Partner A: The behavior I will practice is:	
Partner A: The support I may need is:	
Partner B: The pattern I am working to change is:	
Partner B: The behavior I will practice is:	
Partner B: The support I may need is:	
Shared growth commitment: The pattern we are working to change together is:	
The behavior we will practice together is:	
The way we will review progress is:	

LONG TERM LEARNING AGREEMENT

EXERCISE 8.6

Before You Begin
Create an agreement for how the relationship will keep learning after this workbook.

Prompt	Reflection Space
We agree that our relationship must keep learning because:	
We agree to continue practicing systems thinking by:	
We agree to continue protecting feedback loops by:	
We agree to continue examining mental models by:	
We agree to continue practicing personal mastery by:	
We agree to continue honoring shared vision by:	
We agree to continue learning under stress by:	
We agree to continue holding relationship review meetings by:	
We agree to seek outside support when:	
Our long-term learning agreement is:	

CHAPTER REFLECTION

EXERCISE 8.7

Before You Begin
Use this space to bring together the full workbook framework and identify the next small step in the right direction.

Prompt	Reflection Space
What did I learn about our relationship resilience?	
What warning signs do we need to take more seriously?	
What strengths should we protect?	
What repair practice needs to become more consistent?	
What shared value should guide our next season?	
What personal growth commitment do I need to honor?	
What relationship practice should continue beyond this workbook?	
What is one small step in the right direction that I can take now?	

CHAPTER COMMITMENT

EXERCISE 8.8

Before You Begin
A resilient relationship is shaped through repeated intentional action. This week, practice one behavior that helps the relationship continue learning.

Prompt	Reflection Space
My small intentional action this week will be:	
I will know I practiced it when:	
One warning sign I will monitor is:	
One protective practice I will support is:	
One repair behavior I will practice if needed is:	
I will review this commitment on:	

CONCLUSION

A resilient relationship is not built by avoiding every strain. It is built by learning how to respond when strain appears. It is built when partners notice warning signs, protect resources, repair harm, practice shared values, and continue choosing intentional action in the present moment. Resilience is not a final destination. It is a living practice.

The work of this chapter brings the workbook together. You have examined the relationship as a system. You have studied feedback loops, mental models, personal mastery, shared vision, team learning, review meetings, and resilience planning. Each discipline matters on its own, but together they create a relationship capable of learning. That is the deeper goal. Not a perfect relationship. Not a conflict free relationship. A relationship that can keep learning.

The pages that follow will help you carry this work forward through the closing note and appendices. Those tools will give you repeatable templates for system mapping, conflict tracking, shared vision planning, relationship review, and resilience practice. The workbook may end, but the learning relationship continues through the choices you make next.

CLOSING NOTE

LOVE THAT KEEPS LEARNING

SECTION FOCUS

A final reflection that brings the workbook framework together and invites the relationship to continue learning beyond these pages.

CLOSING NOTE

LOVE THAT KEEPS LEARNING

:A relationship does not become resilient because it avoids every difficult season. It becomes resilient because it learns how to respond when difficulty arrives. It learns how to notice strain before it becomes rupture. It learns how to listen before feedback turns into resentment. It learns how to question assumptions before old stories become the only truth. It learns how to repair with responsibility, protect what is valuable, and return to shared vision when stress begins to narrow the future.

This workbook began with the idea that the relationship is a system. That idea matters because it changes where attention goes. Instead of treating every conflict as an isolated event, you were invited to examine the patterns beneath the event. Instead of asking only who was right or wrong in a particular moment, you were invited to ask what the relationship has learned to do under pressure. This does not erase accountability. It makes accountability more useful. When a couple can see the system, both partners gain a clearer view of what must be protected, repaired, interrupted, or redesigned.

You have worked through feedback loops, mental models, personal mastery, shared vision, team learning, relationship review meetings, and long-term resilience planning. Each discipline offers a different doorway into the same deeper work. Systems thinking helps you see the pattern. Feedback helps you hear the relationship. Mental models help you understand the stories underneath conflict. Personal mastery helps you become more responsible for how you show up. Shared vision gives the relationship direction. Team learning helps you face stress together. Review meetings give love a rhythm of reflection. Resilience planning helps the relationship continue learning after the workbook is complete.

The goal was never to create a perfect relationship. Perfection is too fragile a goal for real love. Real relationships involve miscommunication, disappointment, stress, fatigue, history, fear, repair, tenderness, and change. The stronger goal is to create a relationship that can keep learning. A learning relationship does not deny pain. It does not minimize harm. It does not pretend that love alone can solve every pattern. It becomes willing to observe, name, repair, adjust, and practice again.

There may have been exercises you completed easily and others you resisted. Pay attention to both. The exercises that felt easy may reveal existing strengths. The exercises that felt uncomfortable may reveal areas where the relationship needs deeper care. Discomfort does not always mean something is wrong. Sometimes it means the work has moved close to something important. Growth often begins where the old system begins to feel visible.

As you leave this workbook, remember that insight is not the same as change. Insight begins the process, but practice carries it forward. A single conversation may bring clarity, but repeated intentional action teaches the relationship a new pattern. One apology may soften a moment, but consistent repair rebuilds trust. One shared vision statement may inspire hope, but daily decisions reveal whether that vision is alive. One review meeting may open the door, but a repeated rhythm of review keeps the relationship from drifting back into silence.

Return to these pages when the relationship changes. Return after conflict. Return during stress. Return when you feel distant. Return when things are going well and you want to protect what is working. A learning relationship does not use reflection only when something is broken. It uses reflection as maintenance, as prevention, as alignment, and as a practice of care.

If there is one idea to carry forward, let it be this: resilience is the choice to show up through intentional actions in the present moment. It is not built in theory. It is built in the next conversation, the next repair, the next pause, the next act of honesty, the next small step toward the right direction. The relationship becomes stronger not because the work is easy, but because both partners become willing to keep learning how to love with greater clarity, responsibility, and courage.

Love that keeps learning does not remain the same. It deepens. It matures. It becomes more honest. It becomes more capable of holding pressure without losing itself. It becomes less dependent on illusion and more grounded in practice. This is the work of a learning relationship. This is the work that continues after the final page.

APPENDICES

REUSABLE TOOLS FOR CONTINUED RELATIONSHIP LEARNING, REVIEW, AND RESILIENCE.

SECTION FOCUS

Use these templates after the workbook chapters to repeat the practices that matter most for your relationship system.

APPENDIX A

RELATIONSHIP SYSTEM MAP

Section Focus
Use this appendix when you want to step back and examine the relationship as a whole system. This tool can be revisited whenever the relationship enters a new season, faces stress, or begins repeating a familiar pattern.

Prompt	Reflection Space
Communication:	
Conflict:	
Stress:	
Money:	
Affection:	
Intimacy:	
Parenting or family responsibilities:	

Household labor:	
Work and career demands:	
Extended family:	
Friendships and social life:	
Spirituality or values:	
Personal growth:	
Health and emotional well-being:	
Repair after conflict:	
What is currently working in this part of the relationship?	

What feels strained, unclear, or repeatedly difficult?	
What pattern do we tend to repeat in this area?	
What does each partner seem to need in this area?	
What do I personally contribute to the strength or weakness of this area?	
What would improvement look like in observable behavior?	
The three areas that most need attention right now are:	
Our relationship system currently tends to:	
We want our relationship system to learn how to:	
One small action that could improve the system this week is:	

APPENDIX B

CONFLICT PATTERN TRACKER

Section Focus
Use this tracker after a recurring conflict or tension. The goal is not to prove who was right. The goal is to identify the sequence so the relationship can learn from it.

Prompt	Reflection Space
Date:	
Conflict or tension:	
What happened first?	
What did I feel?	
What did my partner appear to feel?	
What did I make the situation mean?	
What did I assume about my partner's intention?	
What did I say or do next?	
How did my partner respond?	

What did my partner appear to assume about me?	
How did the conflict end?	
Was there repair?	
What remained unresolved?	
The pattern we repeated was:	
My role in the pattern was:	
My partner's role in the pattern appeared to be:	
The feedback signal we may have missed was:	
The mental model or assumption that may have been activated was:	
The personal mastery skill I needed was:	
The repair that may still be needed is:	
The next time this pattern appears, I can interrupt it by:	

APPENDIX C

FEEDBACK LOOP AUDIT

Section Focus
Use this appendix when the relationship feels stuck around repeated complaints, ignored concerns, defensiveness, or emotional distance.

Prompt	Reflection Space
Concern being raised:	
Who is raising the concern?	
How is the concern usually communicated?	
How is the concern usually received?	
What does the listener usually hear?	
What does the speaker usually mean?	
What emotional need is underneath the feedback?	
What defensive response usually appears?	
What happens after the defensive response?	
Does the feedback lead to understanding?	

Does the feedback lead to changed behavior?	
Does the feedback disappear without follow-up?	
Does the same concern return later?	
The feedback loop breaks when:	
The feedback loop could stay open if:	
A clearer way to express the concern is:	
A better way to receive the concern is:	
One question we can ask before defending is:	
One agreement we can make is:	
We will review this feedback loop on:	

APPENDIX D

MENTAL MODEL REFLECTION SHEET

Section Focus
Use this appendix when conflict feels larger than the present event. This tool helps separate what happened from the meaning attached to it.

Prompt	Reflection Space
Situation:	
What happened?	
What did I feel?	
What did I make it mean?	
What story did my mind create?	
What did I assume about my partner?	
What did I assume about myself?	
What did I assume about the relationship?	

What evidence supports this interpretation?	
What evidence does not fully support this interpretation?	
What else could this mean?	
What older experience might this connect to?	
What inherited rule or belief may be influencing me?	
What question could I ask instead of reacting?	
What would a more balanced interpretation be?	
What value do I want to practice in this moment?	
What response would align with that value?	
The mental model I want to notice is:	
The mental model I want to practice is:	

APPENDIX E

SHARED VISION PLANNING SHEET

Section Focus
Use this appendix when the relationship needs direction, realignment, or a clearer sense of what both partners are building together.

Prompt	Reflection Space
The kind of relationship I want to build is:	
The kind of relationship my partner wants to build appears to be:	
The values I most want our relationship to reflect are:	
Value one:	
Value two:	
Value three:	
The values we seem to share are:	
The values we need to discuss more clearly are:	
The part of our relationship vision that feels strongest is:	
The part of our relationship vision that feels unclear is:	

The part of our relationship vision that may create tension is:	
When we are at our healthiest, we:	
When we are under stress, we want to:	
When we disagree, we want to:	
When repair is needed, we want to:	
When making major decisions, we want to:	
Our relationship mission statement is:	
To make this vision visible, we will practice:	
This vision needs to be reviewed on:	

APPENDIX F

WEEKLY RELATIONSHIP REVIEW TEMPLATE

Section Focus
Use this template once a week or as needed. Keep the review focused, respectful, and specific.

Prompt	Reflection Space
Date:	
What felt strong between us this week?	
Where did we feel connected?	
Where did we feel distant?	
What stress affected the relationship this week?	
What feedback signal appeared this week?	
What did we handle well?	
What needs attention before it grows?	
What is one appreciation I want to offer?	

What is one repair I need to make?	
What is one request I want to make clearly?	
What shared value did we practice this week?	
What shared value needs more attention?	
What is one small agreement for the coming week?	
Who will do what?	
When will it happen?	
How will we know it was practiced?	
When will we review it?	
Our next right step is:	

APPENDIX G

RELATIONSHIP RESILIENCE PLAN

Section Focus
Use this appendix to create a long-term plan for protecting and strengthening the relationship system.

Prompt	Reflection Space
Our relationship is strongest when:	
Our relationship is most vulnerable when:	
The patterns that place us at risk are:	
The strengths that protect us are:	
The stressors we need to monitor are:	
Trust:	
Time:	
Emotional safety:	
Affection:	
Shared meaning:	

Financial stability:	
Health:	
Social support:	
Confidence in repair:	
Our early warning signs are:	
A warning sign we tend to minimize is:	
A warning sign that usually appears before conflict is:	
A warning sign that usually appears before distance is:	
When we notice emotional distance, we will:	
When we notice repeated irritability, we will:	
When we notice avoidance, we will:	
When we notice decreased affection, we will:	
When we notice unresolved conflict, we will:	

Our repair ritual will include:	
Our protective practices are:	
Daily practice:	
Weekly practice:	
Monthly practice:	
Stress practice:	
Our long-term learning agreement is:	
We will seek outside support when:	
Our relationship resilience statement is:	

APPENDIX H

WHEN PROFESSIONAL SUPPORT MAY BE NEEDED

Section Focus
This workbook is designed for education, reflection, communication, and relationship development. It can help individuals and couples notice patterns, clarify assumptions, strengthen feedback, create shared vision, and build resilience practices. However, a workbook cannot replace professional support when the relationship involves safety concerns, severe distress, or patterns that require trained intervention.

Prompt	Reflection Space
One or both partners feel unsafe.	
One or both partners avoid honesty because they fear retaliation.	
Conflict includes insults, threats, intimidation, or physical harm.	
One partner controls access to money, transportation, communication, or social support.	
One or both partners experience ongoing trauma responses during conflict.	
Apologies occur repeatedly without meaningful behavioral change.	

The relationship is affected by active addiction or untreated mental health concerns.	
A betrayal has occurred and the couple cannot rebuild trust without guidance.	
One or both partners feel hopeless, emotionally numb, or unable to continue the work alone.	
The exercises in this workbook repeatedly lead to escalation rather than reflection.	
Professional support that may help includes:	
Immediate safety steps or emergency resources may include:	
A qualified professional or support resource to contact is:	
Seeking support is an act of resilience because:	

BIBLIOGRAPHY

Argyris, C. (1977). Double loop learning in organizations. Harvard Business Review, 55(5), 115–125.

Argyris, C., & Schön, D. A. (1978). Organizational learning: A theory of action perspective. Addison-Wesley.

Beck, J. S. (2021). Cognitive behavior therapy: Basics and beyond (3rd ed.). Guilford Press.

Bodenmann, G. (2005). Dyadic coping and its significance for marital functioning. In T. A. Revenson, K. Kayser, & G. Bodenmann (Eds.), Couples coping with stress: Emerging perspectives on dyadic coping (pp. 33–49). American Psychological Association.

Bowen, M. (1978). Family therapy in clinical practice. Jason Aronson.

Bowlby, J. (1969). Attachment and loss: Vol. 1. Attachment. Basic Books.

Candel, O. S., & Turliuc, M. N. (2019). Insecure attachment and relationship satisfaction: A meta-analysis of actor and partner associations. Personality and Individual Differences, 147, 190–199.

Edmondson, A. C. (1999). Psychological safety and learning behavior in work teams. Administrative Science Quarterly, 44(2), 350–383.

Epstein, N. B., & Baucom, D. H. (2002). Enhanced cognitive-behavioral therapy for couples: A contextual approach. American Psychological Association.

Fredrickson, B. L. (2001). The role of positive emotions in positive psychology: The broaden-and-build theory of positive emotions. American Psychologist, 56(3), 218–226.

Hazan, C., & Shaver, P. (1987). Romantic love conceptualized as an attachment process. Journal of Personality and Social Psychology, 52(3), 511–524.

Hayes, S. C., Strosahl, K. D., & Wilson, K. G. (2012). Acceptance and commitment therapy: The process and practice of mindful change (2nd ed.). Guilford Press.

Hobfoll, S. E. (1989). Conservation of resources: A new attempt at conceptualizing stress. American Psychologist, 44(3), 513–524.

Javadivala, Z., Allahverdipour, H., Asghari Jafarabadi, M., Azimi, S., Gilani, N., & Chattu, V. K. (2021). Improved couple satisfaction and communication with marriage and relationship programs: Arc there gender differences? A systematic review and meta-analysis. Systematic Reviews, 10, Article 178.

Johnson, M. D., Lavner, J. A., Mund, M., Neyer, F. J., & Bradbury, T. N. (2021). Within-couple associations between communication and relationship satisfaction over time. Journal of Family Psychology, 36(2), 197–207.

Landolt, S. A., Weitkamp, K., Roth, M., Bodenmann, G., & Kaiser, A. (2023). Dyadic coping and mental health in couples: A systematic review. Clinical Psychology Review, 106, Article 102344.

Ogolsky, B. G., & Bowers, J. R. (2013). A meta-analytic review of relationship maintenance and its correlates. Journal of Social and Personal Relationships, 30(3), 343–367.

Rusu, P. P., Nussbeck, F. W., Leuchtmann, L., & Bodenmann, G. (2020). Stress, dyadic coping, and relationship satisfaction: A longitudinal study disentangling timely stable from yearly fluctuations. PLOS ONE, 15(4), Article e0231133.

Senge, P. M. (2006). The fifth discipline: The art and practice of the learning organization (Rev. ed.). Doubleday/Currency.

Smith, P. (2026). Exploring marital resilience through the lived experiences and perception of spousal support during events of shared stressors (Order No. 32669734) [Doctoral dissertation, Walden University]. ProQuest Dissertations & Theses Global.

Smith, P. (2026). The Learning Relationship: How to See Love as a System and Build One That Can Grow. Beyond Publishing.

Stanton, M. (2012). Systemic thinking in couple and family psychology research and practice. Couple and Family Psychology: Research and Practice, 1(1), 14–30.

Sternberg, R. J. (1986). A triangular theory of love. Psychological Review, 93(2), 119–135.

ABOUT THE AUTHOR

PRINCE-JAMES SMITH, PHD

Prince-James Smith, PhD, is a cognitive psychology scholar, behavioral science practitioner, business strategist, and entrepreneur whose work centers on translating psychological and behavioral principles into practical real-world solutions. He holds a PhD in Cognitive Psychology, a Master of Science in Psychology, a Master of Philosophy in Psychology, and a Bachelor of Science in Business Administration and Change Management.

Dr. Smith's professional background spans business analytics, entrepreneurship, human resources, behavioral intervention, and applied psychology. He has more than thirteen years of experience in business analytics, more than ten years of experience as a human resources manager, and more than a decade of entrepreneurial experience developing businesses from the ground up. His work has consistently focused on systems, decision-making, human behavior, personal development, and the practical application of psychology to everyday life.

His academic and professional interests have long centered on relationships, communication, resilience, and the ways individuals develop within interpersonal systems. His master's thesis focused on improving couple communication techniques, while his doctoral dissertation examined marital resilience through the lived experiences and perceptions of spousal support during events of shared stressors. This scholarly foundation informs his broader work on helping individuals and couples understand how relationships function under pressure and how intentional learning can strengthen long-term connection.

Dr. Smith's approach integrates cognitive psychology, behavioral science, business principles, systems thinking, and relationship research. He is especially interested in how shifting perception can change behavior, improve communication, and support resilience. Through his writing and professional work, he encourages readers to examine themselves and their relationships with clarity, responsibility, and practical intention.

The Learning Relationship Workbook reflects Dr. Smith's commitment to bridging academic knowledge and real-life application. It was created for individuals and couples who want more than inspiration. It was created for readers who are willing to study the patterns of love, practice repair, build shared vision, and continue learning how to show up with purpose.

www.ingramcontent.com/pod-product-compliance
Lightning Source LLC
LaVergne TN
LVHW070910210926
848482LV00017B/1043